FINDING LIGHT IN UNEXPECTED PLACES

COVID-19 Edition

Volume 2

Edited by Maria Jerinic
& Erik Pihel

Palamedes

San Francisco

Palamedes Publishing

www.palamedes.pub

San Francisco

Cover by Lorna Rae Daniel

www.lornaraephotography.com

ISBN 978-0-9996930-1-8

LCCN 2021953072

Also available in ebook:

Kindle d19e516c-23ba-484e-9da6-847a7f4c123e

EPUB a5d22e7a-8c02-4ab6-818d-716939ff15e1

www.palamedes.pub/books/finding-light-2

www.facebook.com/PalamedesPub

www.twitter.com/PalamedesPub

www.instagram.com/PalamedesPub

Editors' Note

Due to the global nature of the COVID-19 pandemic, we chose to honor the style guidelines from the writer's country rather than imposing the style of the United States—where the book was published—on every essay.

Introduction

The COVID-19 pandemic was arguably the first event in human history that affected every person on the planet. A virus from Wuhan, China traveled across the globe into every city, town, village, farm, and mountain top: a nursing home in Iceland; a jungle in Brazil; a hut in India; a research station in Antarctica. The Greek word *pándemos* means "belonging to all the people," and the COVID-19 pandemic belonged to everyone. It showed, in dramatic fashion, how we're all connected.

As it silently and invisibly spread across the globe, leaving mass graves in its wake, many had difficulty adjusting to such a dramatic shift. The disease's effects were quite visible to doctors, nurses, and patients in Intensive Care Units, but for most of us, we caught only indirect hints when we had to change our routines by avoiding public places, working from home, and wearing masks. Changing our behavior pointed to an invisible tragedy.

We like stability, routines, and a feeling that we're in control, but COVID-19 triggered a world-wide feeling of a loss of control. It reawakened our sense of mortality, hardly ever a pleasant realization, and some reacted by downplaying what we couldn't see. For many of us, wearing a mask and getting vaccinated meant acknowledging that we were in real danger. We wore masks to stop our exhalations from infecting others, but our masks were also communication devices. They said to others, *I care about you; I want to protect you; I want you to be safe.* The simple act of strapping on a mask told fellow shoppers and passersby that we'd look out for each other, that we were all in this together.

The truth is that we're radically connected as Doctor Li Wenliang in Wuhan knew only too well when he saw how quickly a new virus was spreading among his patients in December 2019. He died trying to contain it because the health of his patients, his city, and the entire Earth mattered more to him than his own life. He saw things clearly. He understood a fundamental truth: we're not disconnected individuals no matter how isolated or lonely. The pandemic belongs to everyone, and we all belong to each other.

Tragedies often bring communities together, but for this tragedy, we were forced to stay apart. Nevertheless, there were moments of deep connection. In this essay collection, doctors and nurses risk infection to care for the dying gasping for air; patients battle for their lives; and ordinary people discover extraordinary pockets of light in a time of darkness.

Light is infectious. When someone pays for the next driver in a drive-through lane, the recipient is surprised and often wants to repeat the gesture for the next driver. When we hear someone laughing in pure joy, it makes us happy, and we might even laugh ourselves for no reason other than hearing another person's happiness. These small gestures start localized, but perhaps one day they'll turn into a joy for everyone, a *pándemos*, belonging to all the people.

Don & Doff: Finding Light on the Frontlines

Ariana Incorvati, BSN RN

Boston, Massachusetts, USA

It is March 19th, 2020. I will never forget his name, but I will call him Mr. A. His fragile skin is like paper, draping the bones that construct the tiny frame of a body once strong and well-nourished. The laugh lines engraving his face are evidence of his time on Earth well-spent, and his warm smile mismatches his wide eyes ridden with defeat. He is alone and isolated. Every time I walk by his room, I wave at him through the glass, and he struggles between breaths to smile and return the gesture.

My first night taking care of this man, he is completely awake and talks to me in short sentences between labored breaths over the whooshing of oxygen circulating into his lungs. He is on a non-rebreather mask, a face mask designed to deliver air with high concentrations of oxygen, up to 100%. A patient on the non-rebreather is never a good sign because once this effort fails, the only option left is a transfer to the Intensive Care Unit for intubation and use of a ventilator. The robust non-rebreather mask consumes nearly the entirety of his face and presses tightly against his fragile skin. He is inhaling the highest amount of supplemental oxygen possible yet still struggling to breathe and maintain his oxygen saturation levels at a number

4

compatible with life. Somehow, he muddles through the hours of the night, not quite surrendering his fight just yet, and I leave his bedside this morning feeling uneasy.

Leave my work shoes at the front door.

Drop my work bag.

Toss my contaminated scrubs into the laundry.

Head straight for the shower.

Let the hot water sear my skin and cleanse away the
    bleakness of the night.

Collapse into my bed, the only safe space I feel I have
    left.

And finally, as my head hits the pillow, think of Mr.
    A and wonder if he will still be there when I
    return.

Upon arriving the following evening, I glance at Mr. A through the glass window to his room and cannot help but question if this is the same person I had been talking and even laughing with just twelve hours prior. His eyes are now sealed shut, and his body now seems completely lifeless despite the occasional rise and fall of his weary chest. I learn that he is now on comfort measures only, meaning that the focus of his care is making him comfortable rather than curing his illness. The day nurse who cared for him informs me that he came to this decision on his own. Knowing the severity of his condition, he has peacefully surrendered to this beast of a virus. It is now our job to help him in his transition out of this life.

When planning my evening med passes, my gut tells me to see him first. I peep through the window and notice his tense facial expression and jaw opening to gasp air every few irregular breaths. I get the pain medication that he is due for, and I complete my routine of donning my Personal Protective Equipment (PPE).

Feel the burn of alcohol emulsifying the dehydrated skin of my cracked hands.

Don gown and gloves.

Press an old soggy re-purposed N95 mask to my face to inhale the smell of chemicals embedded in its unraveling fibers.

Lastly, pull down my face shield, the finishing touch to the ensemble of PPE armor.

Take a moment to check and make sure I have everything I need.

Crack open the door.

Hear the urgent blaring of the negative pressure alarm for the split second during which I must slink on through and abruptly shut it behind me, sealing myself up to become one with the unknown.

"Hi Mr. A. It's Ariana, your nurse from last night. I brought you some medicine to make you more comfortable." No response. No flicker of the eyelids, no whirring of the oxygen that sustained him the night prior. I am met with mere silence interrupted by the occasional puffs of air struggling to penetrate the alveoli of his distressed lungs. All that was in the hospital bed was the shell of who he was. I attempt to count his respirations, scared that every breath may be the last.

I rub his arm. "This is just some pain medicine, okay?" I always talk to my patients even if they are unresponsive because they lack so much power and control, and I feel the obligation to pick up the pieces. I try my best to fill the void by explaining every single thing that I do. Whether it be, "I'm just going to check your blood pressure and then give you your medicine" or "Let's put some extra pillows under your legs to elevate them." I realize that it is only human nature to feel compelled to dissolve uncomfortable silence, even if that means having a conversation with myself. If the patients can still hear me, I want whatever they hear to be comforting.

I administer the Dilaudid slowly through Mr. A's IV and watch his facial expression relax. I hover at the foot of the bed for what feels like hours, waiting, watching, hoping for his chest to rise once more. I watch the clock and allow the minute hand to make about three breathless rotations before I finally place my stethoscope on his hollow chest. I hear no heartbeat. I hold his wrists to check a pulse. I feel nothing. I place the oxygen probe on his finger to validate these findings, only to see the blue flatline flashing across the monitor. He passed away not even twenty minutes into my shift.

I feel immense guilt for giving that last dose of pain medication that may have stopped his heart, even though his wishes were to die peacefully and pain-free. I tell myself that I did all that I could to care for him, but I can't bring myself to leave him just yet. I stay in his room to complete my documentation as I think about who this man was and all who must have loved him. I say a silent prayer. I tell him I'm so sorry. I rub his head.

Not even an hour later, I tag his toe with his medical identification and place his body into a white plastic zip-up bag with the help of my coworkers. Per infection control policy, we wipe the exterior of the bag with bleach. We take our patients to the morgue ourselves. I am in my full PPE and lock eyes with several other hospital workers on the journey down to this solemn place, the gurney wheels screeching incessantly, drawing attention to one of the first of many lives lost to COVID-19. One doctor shakes her head with sympathy and utters the very words everyone is thinking, "Oh no, here we go." I nod in acknowledgement, reaffirming the unspoken understanding that this is only the beginning of what the upcoming months will bring. The transport worker opens the heavy doors of the giant walk-in refrigerator, and we slide the bag onto the shelf, as if he has a designated spot awaiting his arrival. I sign some paperwork validating his identity and my role as his nurse at his time of death. After saying one last silent goodbye, I return back to the unit. After all, I still have ten more hours of my shift left.

Rip gown and gloves off in one swift motion, peeling away the blanket of emotions attached to it.

Sanitize hands.

Put on new gloves.

Remove my face shield.

Feel the beads of the stinging sweat drip into my eyes.

Remove N95 mask.

Sanitize hands once more.

Put on a surgical mask.

Put on new gloves because the sanitizing wipes I am about to use are toxic to my skin.

Wipe down the face shield and any other surfaces I feel compelled to.

Wipe off the condensation on my glasses that I have

trained my eyes to look beyond for the last

few hours.

Remove gloves.

Wash my hands as long as I need for me to feel okay.

Shed a tear if time permits.

Take a breath.

Move on to the next one.

Repeat.

Don and doff, don and doff. Sometimes I turn this practice into a moment of silent meditation and intention-setting. *What am I going into this patient's room for? What do I want to accomplish? How can I be in and out as quickly yet efficiently as possible? How can I bring some light to this person's very dark reality?* I am learning quickly that in some unfortunate cases, bringing light is simply helping patients to peacefully transition out of the natural world with dignity and grace, just like with Mr. A.

I am a baby nurse, but not the kind who takes care of tiny humans; I am a baby nurse in the sense that I am barely one year into my practice. There are times when I feel invincible and am beaming with pride to be a part of this incredible profession, but a lot of the time, I feel inadequate. Unfit. Useless. Naive. Sub-par. Unequipped. After any end-of-life situations that I face in my job, I often find myself stuck in a pessimistic state of mind, questioning how and why some people end up suffering so much. When I am at home, I try to be present and not think about work, but there are some patients that I cannot get out of my head. The fearful voices of their families, whether they be in person or over Zoom. The growing disappointment in the patients' eyes. Their coming to terms with their poor prognosis. Their desire to no longer live in pain. Their will to move on. My conflicting feelings of both failure and peace of mind when helping them do so with grace. I think of Mr. A often, and as the weeks have turned into months and now a whole year later, I am finally beginning to grasp the reality that my job isn't solely about saving lives; it's about honoring them in whatever way that may be. I realize that, regardless of the outcome, that is often enough.

I used to see all of the difficult situations that I have encountered in just one year as experiences that have shattered my innocence and stolen the light from my spirit, but now I view them as ones that have opened my eyes. From having the ability to be present in people's darkest moments, I realize how fortunate I am to have the privilege to make a difference in some small way. I am more thankful for all of the glimmers of light in my own life, most importantly, the ability to breathe deeply and with ease. Although the circumstances of a global pandemic are terrifying, uncertain, and discouraging, they are also humbling, sobering, and intriguingly inspiring. Seeing so much darkness in this last year has shown me how to let light in by using my position to impact the lives of others in a positive way despite the hardships they may face. Working on the frontlines of COVID-19 has reaffirmed that nursing is my calling, and that it is during the difficult times that we have the most influence on the people we touch. We have a special job: a duty to help the light penetrate through the cracks in the darkest and most broken of places so it can find a home in the hearts of those who ache for it most.

What We Call Grief

Trisha Paul

Minneapolis, Minnesota, USA

In the early days of spring, I spent the lengthening daylight hours distracted by ever-blinking lights and boisterous beeping in the Pediatric Intensive Care Unit (PICU) while the world outside the hospital was quickly becoming a place I no longer recognized. The proximity of others was suddenly filled with great peril. Social rituals like meeting up for coffee, grabbing dinner, or getting drinks were no longer safe, the daily grind of commuting and afterschool activities swiftly dismantled. Our nation, our planet, had been struck by pandemia.

As though an approaching thunderstorm raged outside my window, those first few weeks of March held so much noise. The news rumbled, deep and ominous. Groans of thunder in the distance grew louder as the horror approached, uncertain and hesitant at first but inescapable. From the dim innards of the hospital, I googled "COVID Minneapolis" every day. Even physicians like me were searching for knowledge, shamelessly scouring the internet for answers and striving to understand everything we could about this mysterious virus. We were waiting anxiously for science to catch up with its spread.

In caring for critically ill children with cancer, I was afraid. Without immune systems, my patients were

13

defenseless against all types of infection and presumably even more vulnerable to COVID-19. If their lives depended on immunosuppressive medications, would getting COVID mean delaying and compromising their cancer treatment? With each internet search, I was trying desperately to make sense of an unfolding tragedy I found to be terrifyingly unintelligible. It seemed absurd to be forced to face these kinds of chilling clinical conundrums with so little known about the virus.

Oh, the vertigo of it all. The sensation reminded me of my days as a ballerina, when no amount of spotting could stop the disorientation of twirling. But what was there to fix my gaze upon if the Earth was spinning along with me? I felt as though tectonic plates were shifting beneath my feet, leaving me lurching to maintain my balance, searching for solid ground to stand upon. How were we supposed to keep walking when the ground was crumbling at our feet?

Each day brought new discouragement as the dark lingering from a temperate winter suppressed an emerging spring. As a writer at heart, I often curled up with a notebook and pen at night, trying to gather my thoughts and process the many feelings that accompany medical training. Now I hunched over my laptop and stared at the endless white emptiness behind blinking cursors, waiting for words. I found none. Why were clouds so abundant, and where was the sun when we most needed the light?

Shaken from within, I couldn't remember a time when I

had felt the entropy of the universe so viscerally. Never before had words failed to find me when I so desperately needed them.

When March was coming to an end, on an eerily quiet night in the PICU, I wrote: *This is what we call grief.* With glassy eyes, I watched a revelation materialize before me. I found relief in finding a name for what I had been feeling all along. I said the word *grief* in my mind once more, tasting within the gruff of the word something delicate, something soft.

Finding a word for what I was feeling during a pandemic felt like discovering *terra firma* beneath my feet amid a rough and rocky terrain. I felt steady for the first time since the pandemic had begun and grounded by grief. Grief embraced me, validating the solemnity of my sorrow. I found comfort in the concept of grief, as though the word granted me implicit permission to despair. Of course, I was grieving; of course, we were all grieving. So much had been lost so suddenly that it would have been inhumane *not* to be overwhelmed by grief.

And now, an entire spring of plans uncoiled. Conferences cancelled, concerts postponed. A high school reunion trip no longer possible. When would I see my parents again, my brother? An imagined writing sabbatical abroad became inconceivable. Would I ever see my former lover in Ireland or my dying grandfather in India again? Grief justified my morose and melancholic mood, the restlessness of a mind trapped within an aching and exhausted body. What now was there to look forward to?

Pandemic comes from the Greek word *pándemos*, or "belonging to all the people." COVID-19 cast a shadow upon all of us, entirely disrupting the lives of people of all age groups. More than a million lives lost, with immeasurable losses amongst the living. I was not alone in this suffocating grief, I suddenly realized. The grief was universal, and just like COVID, it belonged to us all.

Collectively, we were angry, and we were sad, confused and worried, yet grief lingered unnamed in the shadows. We huddled alone with our grief in the dark.

In the PICU, my two-year-old patient with cancer rested her head on a pillow covered in clumps of matted blonde hair. Her lungs were failing, and she couldn't breathe on her own. Her dad believed that her lungs were just sleeping, and that all we needed to do was wake them up. He slept in his car, because only one visitor was allowed at the bedside due to pandemic precautions. *Frozen 2* played on repeat in her room, and I heard Elsa mourning soulfully about how "grief has a gravity."

There's a gravity to grief indeed, I thought to myself. Something strong and almost magnetic about its pull. Something reliable in its seriousness and persistence. Buried within grief, however, is something delicate, something soft. Like hot molten lava trapped within the earth's cool crust, that heterogeneity to grief enables an incredible coexistence. Grief's malleability creates a possibility of unburdening.

An analogy grounds me these days. Three same-sized balls placed within three jars, each jar slightly larger from left to right. Pristine and preserved, the balls represent grief: ever-present, everlasting. The jars symbolize all that is life; just as the jars become larger, so too can one's life and world grow to accommodate grief. What a liberalizing realization, to know that I don't have to erase the pain of loss and instead can create new ways of embedding it within my core.

The existence of tragedies like COVID—fraught with inequity, tainted by overpoliticization, cumulating in widespread disruption, devastation, and preventable death—will never make sense to me. But grief makes sense. Grief offers something in the face of adversity, a human mechanism for survival. A way to make sense out of the nonsensical. Sometimes when everyday miracles for my patients become overshadowed by heinous developments in their clinical courses, caring for the ill numbs me. In knowing grief, I am empowered to feel the throes of sorrow that accompany the ecstasies of exhilaration, to silently and loudly suffer and rejoice, to mourn and to celebrate it all. We do not have to be haunted by our greatest moments of grief but rather can be enlightened—even strengthened—by power derived in the darkest of times.

I find that with deliberate intention, I can rest peacefully within this senselessness. If we accept the irrational as integral to the entropy of our universe, then maybe we can make do. Within the excavation and emptiness of grief, we can find a way to feel whole once more.

None of Us Could See

Amir Farid

Sacramento, California, USA

The tintinnabulation of my pager roused me at half past midnight from what had become my routine raucous slumber. (Once restful reprieves were now a battlefield of worry, simulated exercises for what could happen in the coming days of a pandemic we now existed in...or existed for I suppose.) This tone was quickly becoming a symphony of nightmares. The sound it conjured meant that some unfortunate soul was suffering from a heart attack in the emergency room. "Time to go," I grumbled.

I threw off my covers and summoned some small semblance of resolve. I found my keys, wallet, and white coat with some haste and abandoned the safety of my home. What made my upcoming sojourn to the hospital particularly troubling was a new menace that had invaded our lives, SARS-CoV-2 the novel causative organism of COVID-19. This master of maladies' initial claim-to-fame was the compromising effect it had on the lungs, but there was also growing evidence that it could be a trigger of myocardial infarctions (heart attacks).

Some months before that fitful awakening, we heard whispers of war from across the Pacific Ocean. A novel pathogen was waging a frightful campaign in China. The people were locked down in their homes in what seemed to be an endless siege. Our own media reported that the mysterious situation was being monitored. Be calm and carry on with our lives was the general message.

We were fools! Fools to think it had been contained. Fools to think we could comprehend it all. The details coming out at best were hazy approximations of reality. The data was as reliable as rumor. It was said that flu-like symptoms predominated. It was said children seemed to be safe. All the while we still awaited any sliver of suggestion about mortality rate. At the time, the CDC told the public it was their duty not to wear masks and save those for healthcare providers...we know better now I suppose.

For most of us practicing medicine, we are used to changing paradigms in the field, but this state of being, this emerging knowledge base, was truly mercurial. Life now had all the predictability of an M. C. Escher painting. Also disconcerting at the start of the pandemic was that we could not pinpoint how the disease was spread; maybe we still can't. In addition to the struggles of day-to-day life was the constant unknown on the frontlines. Was it airborne, i.e., hovering for long periods of time in the breathable air and over longer distances in very small particles? Was it droplet, i.e., only spread in larger particles and over a short distance? That kind of knowledge was crucial to protecting providers and patients in the hospital as it determined precautions we took when going into the patient's room. These were the thoughts that assaulted me that night I drove to hospital to evaluate the case.

I arrived at the emergency room (ER) eleven minutes after the pager sounded. The environment of the ER had metamorphized to a new normal. Providers adorned in personal protective equipment (PPE) rushed around the halls. Draped in blue they ran...sapphire specters, azure apparitions. I weaved through them and made my way to the resuscitation room. The goggles, the N95 mask, the gown, the foot covers, the armor, the ritual. I entered the room to begin our discussion with plans to eventually relay to the patient that I was concerned she was having a heart attack based on her electrocardiogram (ECG), and we'd need a left cardiac catheterization to investigate and treat her. (The cardiac catheterization, also referred to as a coronary angiogram, is an invasive procedure where we use dye to look for any blockages in the arteries that feed the heart, then open them up if we find them.)

As always, the patient encounter began with her chief complaint, which she fearfully told me was: "Fever." *What fever!?* I thought to myself. *You are supposed to say "chest pain!" No one said anything about a fever!* She expounded upon this: a cough, muscle aches, and sore throat for the preceding three days before the chest pain started.

Now I'm the only cyan spirit in the room; the rest had backed away. *Don't get distracted!* I thought to myself; *she is still having a heart attack.* Wait, but was she? We had

21

heard numerous reports of false cases, cardiac catheterization labs activated and staff exposed, all to find out it was the virus up to one of its tricks. Yet, there were real heart attacks too. You could not tell until the patient was on the procedure table (the table of truth) and had their arteries interrogated. Could the virus cause heart attacks? The limited signs pointed to yes. By another turn of the screw of life's cruelty, the virus triggered the body to release inflammatory mediators that dissolved and ruptured cholesterol plaques leading to a heart attack. We had to go on.

I explained the procedure, got her signature on the consent form for permission to do the heart catheterization, and called the cardiologist. "Dr. W., we need to activate the cardiac catheterization lab," I said.

He responded, "I know, I got the call and will be there in five minutes."

"I need to tell you something," I went on. "The patient reports three days of fever." I could almost hear him become tense. The patient had just received her diagnostic COVID-19 swab, but we could not wait for the results...time was heart muscle.

"You know there were some published false cases..." he reassured me.

"I know, but the ECG is hard to ignore," I responded. We decided to proceed. The staff was dressed in the appropriate attire of the evening. The room where we performed the procedure already had the infectious precautions with the deafening din of the air filter to keep us company during the procedure. *It'll be okay,* I told myself. *Just another case.*

Back then, no one knew how to safely proceed. We all had gowns. We all wore N95 masks but covered them with surgical masks just so we could reuse the precious N95 masks later. I wore goggles, but now I could not see through the fog of my own making. Should I wait for a special respirator? *No time,* I thought. I put down the goggles, picked up a face shield and started the case. With a fear I rarely felt before, my heart raced to match my patient's, and the case went on. The heart attack was real. Her obstructed artery was no more by the end...but there was still that other thing. Did she have COVID-19? The COVID-19 test was collected and the word "pending" kept dogmatically appearing as we refreshed the results page of her electronic medical chart over and over again.

I sent the patient to recover in the Intensive Care Unit, and she walked out of the hospital four days later. Twenty-four hours after the case, the results of her COVID-19 test came back negative. She was lucky, as were we. Such was this case, but what about the next? Already pessimism permeated my thoughts.

Pessimists are just practical realists. National borders are imaginary. When the first cases were detected abroad, we should have anticipated the inevitability of their arrival.

Now we are left in the new normal. Are there any silver linings in these clouds? The darkness was everywhere and, at times, overwhelming. The goal was to go on, to persist...persistence was not futile. Adjust to the new normal, this walking and waking dream state. The new goal was to continue going through the nightmare. It was as Winston Churchill said, "If you're going through hell, keep going." Every day was another jaunt into the unknown, once more into the nightmare factory. What of those "essential workers," those who more often travail the dark? What of first responders, hospital staff, community pharmacists, farmers and laborers, store clerks, cooks, factory works, and others?

At least now a new light has shown on the endeavors of such individuals. With this new blight we've seen how truly dependent we are on our fellow human beings. The Irish poet W. B. Yeats once pondered about the driving force that led a young airman to a "tumult in the clouds." What drove any essential worker out of their homes? Was it a sense of duty? A desire to help humankind? Bills to pay? The word "hero" has been floated around, but does anyone feel like that as they leave the sheltered safety? I felt fear that day both for the patient and for myself. I was glad the mask kept my facial emotions at an apt social distance.

Perhaps there are the occasional lights in the darkness, but I feel my eyes cannot adjust to see them on most days. So many unanswered questions exist, and human unity is needed more now than ever. Is the vaccine the answer? Will the loss of lives stop? Will the economy recover? Can people change their behavior? Can we learn to lean on each other? Can we forgive and support each other's weaknesses? How long can that newfound magnanimous nature last? We all commence our days hoping to match the spinning of the Earth as we are assaulted by tearful statistics. I can only speak of my own emotions, but I find myself falling to sleep as I assume many now do, in prayer for reprieve. Until then, we shall continue on our trek through the fog of war, as do our compatriots. Because of oaths we swore, we shall use the knowledge that we acquired to help humanity in any way we can until one day all of us can both literally and metaphorically emerge from this novel war hand-in-hand.

Disaster Artist

Carlos Hiraldo
Astoria, New York, USA

"You are so relaxed while the city goes insane!" I yelled at Annabel over the phone, somewhat lacking sanity myself. I was worried after my visit to the supermarket that Thursday in early March. Up to then, I had been right there with my wife in dismissing the emerging pandemic as so much media hype, like MERS and Ebola before.

She had taken our boys, Jack and Conrad, to drumming lessons, so it was my night to cook. On a regular weeknight around 4:30 p.m., Key Food on 30th Avenue in Astoria, Queens will have a few customers, most with kids in tow, buying items needed for the evening meal. That Thursday of March 12th 2020, I was stunned by how packed the store was as I stopped on my way home. It was not pandemonium as in apocalyptic movies. There was no yelling, no screaming, no fighting over food items. There was just an atmosphere of mass concentration, an intensity that felt like hard work. The aisles were jammed with single shoppers, filling carts with iterations of the same products: multiple giant toilet rolls, manifold Kleenex boxes, assorted house cleaning products and disinfectants, copious canned goods, and stacks of frozen foods. Slowly swerving my cart around the many solitary shoppers, I noticed more and more empty shelf spaces. Perhaps capitalism would not save us after all.

It mattered very little if I ultimately agreed with Annabel about all the panic shopping being *rubbish*. What mattered was that if everyone believed that the thing to do was to purchase large stocks of supplies as a response to their fears, as they usually do in New York City with predictions of massive snow falls and devastating tropical storms, then we would be left with two hungry, growing boys and no supplies. That argument, articulated in a considerably more passionate tone during our phone conversation, triggered Annabel's motherly instincts. She promised to stop by the supermarket and get more food on her way back with the kids. When I hung up, I was satisfied with myself. I had done all I could with a bag full of books on my back by having purchased, along with the necessary ingredients for the evening meal, an until then totally unnecessary pack of Charmin toilet rolls, and Bounty paper towels to jam into our supply closet.

It was the end of the second week of the semester at the City University of New York (CUNY) community college in which I had been working for eighteen years. As I had done every semester since September 2001, I had scheduled Fridays as a reading and grading day. That evening, I felt that I deserved to unwind by cooking while watching the usual ESPN offering of sports banter shows. I was looking down a fourteen-week long barrel of essay after essay shooting at me. I was not going back to the stores to find myself with the same types who rush to the supermarkets two or three times every winter in response to the trance-inducing media shrill, "It's snooohhwiiiihhng!"

Calling Annabel primarily served as an attempt to transfer my own bewilderment. I remained a refusenik to the competition for durable edibles, but I was now aware of the simmering, brewing panic manifested at the supermarket. The wife, on the other hand, seemed only alert to the rhythmic talents of our pre-pubescent percussionists. Yes, I was passing the buck in a combination of laziness and sanctimonious ass-covering common to husbands and politicians the world-over, but in my defense, I was exhausted by thoughts of another semester stretching before me. Deep down, I still hoped this whole Coronavirus thing, like most things in life, would come to nothing. In fact, by trying to steer Annabel from calm indifference to alarmed intensity, I was engaging in magical thinking. Part of me believed then that if she came back home angry, as opposed to sporting her usual upper-crust English cheerfulness, with arms weighed down by overstuffed grocery bags, and two shell shocked kids in tow, it would increase the likelihood that everything would turn out alright in the end, following, according to my logic (or lack thereof), that law of existence which mandates that most effort exerted will be for naught. In future months, according to my vision, we would open a kitchen cupboard full of canned beans and chickpeas and laugh at the

Thursday in March when we thought our lives would stop.

I was then that incredibly annoying character found in every horror or mass destruction movie who arrogantly refuses to accept the worst and most accurate interpretation of what is happening until it is far too late to escape. You know who I am referring to. He is usually a lanky, white middle-aged male who believes himself rational when he argues preposterous denials of what he and those around him are evidently experiencing. The one who provides audiences with a good amount of *schadenfreude* when he inevitably dies in some undignified manner, like having a bolder or large piece of concrete structure fall from above and squash him flat. At that early stage of the pandemic's arrival in New York City—as I usually am during emerging catastrophic scenarios, as I was on my first day of work on September 11, 2001, when I disbelieved my new colleagues' claims that one plane had also hit the Pentagon and another had been taken down by its passengers on its way to the Capitol Building—I was the husky Latino version of *that* guy.

When Annabel got home exhausted and angry with our shell-shocked boys that Thursday evening, she reaffirmed my skepticism towards the threat by swinging between criticizing me as an overreacting outlier to criticizing American society for addressing all concerns with shopping. Surely, this kind of nonsense was not taking place in her native London. Her dismissal of my panicked tone during our phone conversation and of the society which induced it was slightly tamed by her acknowledgement that the items she had been able to secure, chewy bars, tonic water, digestible cookies, gin, chicken breasts, and frozen fish sticks did not amount to many meals. After we ate the pasta Bolognese I had prepared, we put the kids to bed and sat back to watch TV with some gin and tonic.

§

I look forward to the first couple of Fridays in a semester. The kids go to school, the wife works, and I have no major assignments to grade at that early stage in the semester. But the next day the anticipation of relaxation was quickly marred after dropping the kids off at PS 166 on 35th Avenue. The Starbucks up the avenue was almost empty. That usually relaxes me. Still, I am reasonable. I expect some build-up of customers during the couple of hours I sit there slow reading a book and the news while sipping my caramel macchiato. I was waiting alone while the barista called out name after name, preceded by the words, "mobile order for." News alerts on my phone provided jittery company. The governor of New York State and the mayor of New York City, usually at odds with each other, had insisted in separate morning news conferences that there would be no general shutdown. That sounded both auspicious and suspicious.

As soon as I settled into my window-facing stool, news

updates about my workplace lit up my screen. Intermittent work emails confirmed what the news had reported a beat earlier. First, I learned that CUNY would cancel its study abroad program for the semester. Then, that CUNY would close for two weeks. Alas, by the time I was ready to pack, CUNY had announced it would close all campuses and switch to remote learning for the rest of the Spring semester. I worried about the types of "further details" that my last work email promised would greet us on Monday as we were told to report to an emergency meeting. As I walked out of Starbucks, I realized there had been only sporadic traffic. At no time during my two hours stay had there been more than a handful of customers sitting in the cavernous Queens store. Only the occasional straggler had wondered in, taking a drink to go.

Still, as Annabel would say, it wasn't all *gloomy.* Underneath all that gruff dismissal, the annoying character in disaster films is an incorrigible optimist. I envisioned myself having a less stressful semester than usual after a period of adjustment to online teaching. I imagined leisurely working from home, having long lunches with the wife who, as a consultant for human rights organizations, already worked from home. For the rest of the semester, I would be free from direct contact with the myriad of issues community college students bring to a classroom.

In the meantime, my boys would continue to attend school. Mayor Bill de Blasio had insisted during his Friday morning news conference that "New York City schools will not close." He spoke eloquently about the city's public schools needing to remain open. He described them as an essential pillar of healthcare. He spoke movingly about how tens of thousands of students depended on school breakfasts and lunches as their only nutritious meals of the day. No, according to our mayor, New York City schools could never close.

I accepted this repeated assurance throughout the weekend despite the mayor's and the governor's increasingly dark pronouncements in dueling news conferences. On Saturday morning, the mayor announced restaurants and bars in the city would operate at half capacity as of the following Tuesday. A little later, in his own press conference, Governor Andrew Cuomo insisted that type of decision was only his to make, and he had not come to it yet. By Saturday afternoon, a spokesperson for the governor announced that restaurants and bars throughout the state would operate at 50% capacity as of the following Tuesday. On Sunday morning, the governor announced that non-essential businesses like bars, restaurants, barbershops, and hair salons would close completely. It was not clear whether this dictate included gyms, a concern for many city dwellers, especially our progressive mayor, who infamously got a last workout on Monday morning at his Brooklyn YMCA, taking his SUV motorcade through his usual, unnecessarily long, gas guzzling commute from Gracie Mansion in lower Manhattan to Park Slope, Brooklyn. But on Sunday afternoon, after insisting that New York City schools would never close, Mayor De Blasio speculated that perhaps the whole city should go into lockdown. A spokesperson for Governor Cuomo followed up with a press release that insisted only the governor had the authority to order a lockdown of any municipality within New York State. Despite the various warnings on my iPhone, iPad, and television screens, I went to the kids' soccer practice that evening believing that no matter what happened, New York City schools would remain open.

§

Annabel and I normally stand out for sitting, reading while our kids practice with their soccer club on Sunday nights. It is not that we are uninterested in watching our boys play. It is that we are much more interested in finishing the book or article we are reading than in watching other people's kids play. We will raise our heads intermittently to catch one of our boys make a nice pass or save. And if we miss any of the action, we will studiously pretend to one of our little darlings to have witnessed and cheered his spectacular goal or gravity defying save unless, of course, he catches us *in delicto* in which case we will feign confusion or apologize sincerely as a last resort.

That Sunday night, we blended with the other parents.

We sat at the edge of the narrow metal benches that line the walls of the gym, staring at little screens in semi-hunch. There were still some oblivious types, yelling encouragements to their kids in not exactly PG rated language. But there was much less of that behavior than usual. Whenever I looked up from the screen to recover from some bad breaking news item, I noticed fewer parents overall, as if they were disappearing in mid-practice. A great proportion of those still present had masked faces. Things had changed dramatically from the start of the weekend. By the time soccer practice was done, all New York State schools were closed. We were officially in lockdown.

§

It began with coughs the next morning. I didn't think much of it. We usually all get sick two or three times during winters. Having personally experienced nothing thus far, I thought March was as good a time as any to catch a cough. The kids had been coughing for a couple of days, nothing severe. Annabel too had a slight cough. We had read that little kids weren't susceptible to COVID-19. We thought that if the kids couldn't get sick, then they couldn't transmit it. Anyway, this fit the well-worn pattern of how we caught colds and flus every winter. One boy got sick. Then one parent got sick. Then the other boy caught the same thing. Then the last parent got sick. A couple of weeks later, the first sick boy fell ill again—repeat until May. "So why not go to our favorite neighborhood restaurant for one last meal?" I suggested upon my arrival from the dreary set of meetings at my school.

The nineteen-nineties Will Smith film *Independence Day* is at best a guilty pleasure. You'll enjoy it when you stumble upon it on cable and have nothing to do or, better yet, when you have something that you are avoiding, like a stack of student papers to grade. Afterwards, you will feel bloated even if you had nothing to eat while watching. It is visual junk food, spectacle aiming at nothing but spectacle. Yet, like any narrative, it can stumble upon some veracities of the human experience. In its first act, the movie is rich in annoying, incredulous characters who seem to have an inexhaustible capacity for denying a looming disaster. There is a captivating scene where a group of young optimists turns a skyscrapers' heliport into a night club cum rally to welcome the spaceship that hovers right above them. They dance to loud music, wave placards with positive messages, and scream affections to the alien visitors. The partiers' beatifically raised expressions turn askance when a portal opens from below the ship. Suddenly, electric blue light descends on them and blows up the skyscraper. Now, take away the loud music, the happy, good looking, mostly young crowd, and the welcome signs—that was pretty much us at the restaurant that Monday afternoon. Except the deadliness heading our way was not concentrated in a beam but diffused in the late winter air.

§

Despite agreeing to my invite, as she often does after acquiescing to one of my dubious pleasure-seeking ideas, the human rights consultant and advocate in Annabel would not allow us to enjoy ourselves without a good dosage of moral hectoring. On the way to the restaurant, she expounded on the twin iniquities my suggestion and her prior enthusiastic consent revealed: profligacy with money and recklessness with our family's health. She excoriated, with an intensifying rhetoric that would have made Vladimir Lenin demure, the lifestyle that allowed us to spend money on a restaurant meal at a time when many New Yorkers were losing their jobs due to the imminent shutdown. She also worried our lunch outing added potential health injury to economic insult by putting our family's health and that of the restaurant's staff at risk. I had been determined to get through the one and a half block trek to the restaurant without letting her convince us to turn back home in symbolic solidarity with the newly unemployed. I responded that the restaurant staff, scheduled to follow the next day into unemployment, could benefit from our patronage one last time. As for her healthcare concerns, I quelled her trepidations by arguing that one final outing together would provide the salve our spirits needed prior to a few weeks of lockdown.

Usually at lunch time, even on a gray weekday afternoon, The Grand is packed with a mostly immigrant

36

clientele of thin twenty-something, swarthy-white couples in tight blue jeans, tighter spandex, and geometrically elaborate but perfectly trimmed beards chatting quietly under the incongruently loud Berlin club music. To our surprise, we found the place almost desolate when we entered. The four of us made up the third set of customers in the huge establishment. The silence and emptiness of the restaurant enveloped our family. As we sat at our table, I tried to dispel any second thoughts by looking forward to my pink lemonade. When another family arrived with a little girl around the same age as our youngest, Annabel relaxed a bit. Suddenly, we were not the only family exposing our kids and ourselves to the killer in the air. So I picked up the baton and started getting jittery throughout the course of the meal.

Judging by its American-sized portions and its Old-World service, The Grand expects customers to arrive in the contradictory state of ravenous hunger and meditative patience. Things were taking even longer than usual despite the sparse attendance. As she set the appetizers down, I chatted up the young Eastern European waitress for information. We learned she was the only one serving. The kitchen was short as well, most of the staff having called in sick. After this news, I tried to lighten the mood by half-smiling and asking Annabel, "Hey, why don't we get a couple of martinis?" She smiled back and looked askance, "Really?" This of course is her natural English way of saying, "Yes, please, I would really love to have another drink." She pointed out that, unlike my juice, her Bloody Mary already contained alcohol. I convinced her with the uncontestable argument that she was halfway through her drink. So two martinis it was. This made bearable the slow pace of a meal with angsty kids distracted from iPad surfing by the increasing desolation of an establishment from which customers left without being replaced. We demonstrated great restraint by not ordering second martinis. It helped that the kids surprised us by foregoing their usual Oreo milkshake desserts. By the time we left the restaurant, my cough had subsided, and I felt more relaxed if more aware of the empty streets.

§

Two weeks later, I walked wrapped up in a scarf to the CVS Pharmacy on the corner of 31st Avenue and Steinway Street. I went searching for surgical masks and any cold products I could purchase. The late March sky was a dreary, light gray. The cold was stale, not biting like in January or February. Ambulance sirens punctured the stagnant silence. The block was cleared of the usual retiree *bon vivant* and busybodies. There was not a soul in sight until I turned right and saw a few stragglers coming out of the Associated Supermarket that, like much of my block, remains in the 1970s in terms of style, offerings, and technology. Uphill to Steinway, I kept consciously readjusting my scarf, as it came undone with every new coughing spree.

I felt tired. Teaching online had turned out to be much more challenging than I expected. Only two-thirds of my students had returned after the one-week teaching pause CUNY had set aside to crash train faculty in the dubious arts of online teaching. Yet communicating with the remaining students through email was time consuming and susceptible to misunderstandings. I kept being surprised by how few actually read and processed the material I posted on Blackboard, our government approved teaching site.

CUNY had recommended we teach asynchronous classes. We were to forgo any mandatory videoconference attendance and allow students to work on assignments on their own time as long as they completed each task by the due date. Very few met the first due dates for assignments. We were also encouraged to suggest, not mandate, that students join us for weekly videoconferences during one of the days and times we would have met in the classroom when teaching was done in-person. These were only an hour long per class. They were sparsely attended since many of our students didn't have reliable access to the internet and others pretended they didn't.

The Zoom meetings were also more challenging than I had expected. Like freedom, reliable internet access is an ideal seldom met. We were beset by frozen videos due to internet crashes. I was a consistent culprit in these interruptions as Spectrum WIFI couldn't be trusted to work without multiple interruptions when my two boys, my wife and I used the internet four or five hours a day. Even when the technology worked, videoconferences were awkward. Most students refused to turn on the video feature on their devices, and I didn't feel comfortable asking them to do so. Many students lived in precarious housing, sharing minimal space with numerous relatives and acquaintances. I often found myself talking to my own image, surrounded by recognizable names and weird internet handles inside black boxes. Students rarely asked questions, and when I asked a question of them, most of the time an interminable silence would ensue before I volunteered a reply.

The combination of online teaching and assisting my own kids with online learning could explain my exhaustion, but I felt strange. A muscular pain shot through my body. I hadn't exercised since the start of lockdown and the onset of my cough, but as I walked to the store, I felt the kind of soreness on my thighs, back, and chest that I would normally feel the day after a session of treadmill running and weightlifting at our now closed gym. I had mentally dismissed Annabel's claim that she couldn't smell anything as bandwagon COVID-19 paranoia before setting off. But as I walked the streets, I realized I couldn't even smell the fabric of my knitted scarf. On the way back from the store, sans surgical masks, but, with a semi-successful haul of Advil, Children's Tylenol, NyQuil, and blue surgical gloves that impressed two sets of customers enough to ask me in which aisle I'd found them, I convinced myself there was nothing seriously wrong with me. That frustrating character in disaster films is nothing if not an ad hoc rationalizer. I told myself l couldn't smell anything because there was no one on the streets and nothing to whiff, not even garbage. Like that character, I was about to get my comeuppance.

§

Next day, Tuesday, the boys came into our room at 7:50 a.m. I was alarmed that Annabel and I had woken up so late. On normal days, I let Annabel take the lead and the brunt of the morning routine with the kids. The fever I had developed the night before was still there. Yet Annabel hadn't budged after saying, "I'll be right up." I tossed the sheets and jumped out of bed, annoyed at my own body. A month before, I had been diagnosed with hypertrophic cardiomyopathy. Heart specialists from both NYU Langone and Weill Cornell had recommended that I have a defibrillator implanted "as an insurance." April 9th had been set aside as the tentative date for the procedure. I was scared by what the surgery meant about aging and approaching mortality. I didn't feel any of the symptoms that would make me run towards a defibrillator. Never felt faint, never felt out of breath, and never fainted. I had run the NYC Marathon five years before. And in the span of five months, from September 2019, when I went for my annual physical, to February 2020, I had been pushed from healthy

41

middle age to fragile old age by American doctors who, as one of the specialists admitted, were playing "sort of a numbers game in the US that European doctors, for example, wouldn't necessarily follow." I was not going to let some overhyped, flu-like newbie Coronavirus stop me from being an active father. That incredibly annoying character in disaster films is at heart an American go-getter, believing a little pluck and tough resolve is all it takes.

Almost immediately, I lost the "I'll show them" verve that sprung me from bed. Down the stairs I went, gently and slowly. I squinted at the overhead lights reflecting from my kids' red cereal bowls. My eyelids fell heavier with each blink. I realized I was about to faint. I set the bowls down on the table in front of Jack and Conrad, turned left, and crashed on the sofa. But I didn't lose consciousness. Crunching cereal sounds, usually a pleasant percussive companion to the morning routine, crashed against my eardrums like concrete from a collapsing building. This unbearable noise was punctured by siren wails—the only sound of life from the empty streets. I breathed heavily against the musty cushions. After what seemed like hours, Conrad came to me and said, "Daddy, we're done." I told him, "Get your mom, please, and tell her that I almost fainted."

At these words, Annabel arrived with thermometer in hand. My temperature had increased from the previous night to 100.6. She encouraged me to eat something, but I had barely mustered a sitting position to have my temperature taken. I had no desire for food. She suggested I lie down, but I wouldn't budge until she took her own temperature. She reported that she remained at a 100.4. That was good news. I climbed one step at a time, holding the thick rail banister with both arms, going slowly one over the other, like a mountaineer holding the ropes in a last push to the summit. I lay in bed for a four-day stay.

My temperature rose rapidly for the first two days. This was no flu. Despite doing nothing but the occasional typing in bed, I was sore all over, like I had felt in the last days of training for the marathon. My breathing became increasingly labored. Surreal foreboding carried my thoughts away. I swung back and forth between feeling sorry for my state and worrying about Annabel and the kids. It felt like at any time Annabel would fall as ill as I was. What would happen then to our boys? Despite being a native New Yorker, I had no real family left in the city. Both of us had few close friends. Who besides teachers would be expected to risk Corona to care for other people's kids? At other times, I was convinced that Annabel (downstairs trying to work while helping the kids, stepping out to buy groceries, and cooking while plowing through her own slight fever) was more than happy to see me go. I had vivid images of a house in Wimbledon, a framed picture of me in the second rung of a living room bookshelf as the only evidence I had ever existed, my kids cheerfully referring to a debonair, white-haired Englishman named James as dad. I lost all appetite. For a couple of nights running, a half bowl of supermarket red pepper and smoked gouda soup sufficed for dinner. Meanwhile, regular sounds and light shocked me. The dead sky that blanketed New York City in March and April was a kind of blessing. I dreaded the idea of being sick with COVID-19 on a sunny summer's day.

§

That Tuesday afternoon, I asked Annabel for my laptop. That incredibly annoying, incredulous character in disaster movies would be the strictest of converts, browbeating anyone who didn't adapt to the new conditions quickly enough to his liking if he were lucky enough to survive into the sequel's post-apocalyptic society. I was certain that soon I would be too sick to teach, so I sent an email addressed to my chair and to my union representative, both good friends, excoriating them for various perceived transgressions.

I was convinced that no one at work cared for my plight and that in order to get paid I would have "to fill out the war & pece [sic] length documentation that is normally required." Those were the words I sent my chair and my rep, lashing out at both administration and union. I claimed disbelief that instead of negotiating better working conditions under the circumstances, "the union had found more important things to do like endorsing Bernie Sanders's moribund campaign." Never mind that I too had been an enthusiastic Bernie supporter. Socialized medicine would not come fast enough to rescue me from a New York City where the hospital system verged on collapse. I had forgotten the 160 sick days I had accumulated thanks to my union-bargained contract. Despite my fierce rhetoric, I could barely sit up, propped up by my own pillows and Annabel's. Every other Teflon-smooth clang of the keyboard made me squint in discomfort. Getting out three short paragraphs had taken over an hour.

I didn't see my kids for the rest of the day. I didn't see my kids Wednesday, except for a wave goodbye from the door. Annabel slept on a futon downstairs. Our bed was soaked with my sweat. This was the closest our family came to seriously quarantining, despite having the space that comes with living in an actual house with a garden in New York City as opposed to an apartment.

§

That week, my students had an article to read and an assignment due at the end. But I was certain that by Thursday I would miss my usual Zoom meeting for a date with a ventilator. Wednesday morning, with the previous night's NyQuil worn off, my fever was at 103 degrees. My Primary Care Physician's (PCP) phone wouldn't stop ringing, like all desolate phones must have done before the advent of the answering machine in the 1970s; not even the high-pitched sound of a full digital mailbox disrupted its shrill monotony. I gave up. I sent all my students the following email:

Dear Students,

As some of you are aware, I have been sick for over a week. However, in the past days my health has taken a turn for the worse with fever, perpetual cough, and an inability to tolerate regular sounds and noises. Monday was the last time I communicated with a group of students when I held a Zoom meeting with about five attendees and went over the material I put in the Week 5 folder of the Weekly Content area. That was for my Monday and Wednesday classes. I wanted to offer the same for my Tuesday and Thursday class, but I have been unable to leave my bed since Tuesday.

If I don't turn a corner by the end of this week, I will ask the school to take over my classes and assign them to other instructor/s. This may be a welcomed or unwelcomed possibility, depending on whether you think I am a hardass grader or not. I am amazed at how many students are still worried about their grades as if it was a life-or-death issue, when a life-or-death civilization-threatening pandemic rages through the world right outside their windows. Of course, this mind-blowing lack of perspective still doesn't motivate many of those most concerned about grades to actually try their best in their first submissions of essays and various exercises. But be that as it may, I am trying to hold off from admitting defeat because the moment I surrender my classes, it will become a bureaucratic nightmare for the school and most importantly for you.

So I will try to see if things get better. In the meantime, hold on. Complete the debatable v non-debatable exercise. Submit it. Don't contact me for anything else. I am in no condition to reply to 30 or 40 messages whether they are well-meant or dubiously ignore everything I just stated about my health. I will either contact you when I feel better, or you will be contacted by someone at the school.

Let's hope for the best.

Typing such a long announcement seemed like a day's work. Every clang of the keyboard felt and sounded like a blow to my head. I would like to blame the mixture of self-pity and haranguing in my work missives on what has been variously named COVID-19 Delusion, COVID-19 Paranoia, and COVID-19 Psychosis. Outside, the sirens wailed.

It took me hours to recover after hitting send. I laid there listening to one ambulance after another, at times confusing the intermittent sounds of work from my wife and kids downstairs with a celebration of my impending demise. I covered myself with the sheets, hurting physically and mentally. Every minute that Annabel did not check on me felt like a display of outrageous indifference. Eventually, I harnessed enough strength to ask my cardiomyopathy specialist via email if my condition could be considered a comorbidity. To his credit, I received a call within a couple of hours. His assistant said the doctor didn't believe my condition was a serious risk factor and asked if I had gone to a hospital. Immediately forgetting my gratefulness at being contacted, I testily replied that the news had said people shouldn't go to the hospital if they could breathe on their own. I complained about not being able to contact my PCP and the overall failures of the for-profit U.S. healthcare system. Before hanging up, she suggested I do a telehealth appointment via the NYU Langone app. After a period of lying there breathing and brooding heavily, I got my iPad and booked an appointment with a Dr. Patel for the following evening, one I thought I had good odds of not making.

§

I found myself staring at a "doctor will be right with you" message on the screen an hour past the appointed time. I felt doomed. Civilization had collapsed. Outside, sirens punctured the otherwise eerie silence. Red ambulance lights flashed from below. When she came to check on me,

Annabel told me that an elderly lady who lived five houses away from us had been taken. She asked me if I wanted to come down. For a beat, I thought this was a nefarious question to ask. Part of a plot to zap my diminishing strengths. But I said yes, slowly getting out of bed and making my way downstairs.

I hadn't seen the kids for the better part of three days. Sitting there at a distance from them, I realized how much I had missed them. An ease penetrated my chest as I looked from the TV screen to their faces. I hadn't been able to help them with their homework in a while. I asked them how school was going. Jack spoke about missing friends, while Conrad seemed amazed at how easy a two-hour school day was to complete. Annabel asked if I wanted something to eat. I remembered I had rejected her earlier attempt to bring me lunch. All I had all day was a *malta*, a non-alcoholic dark beer. I suddenly hankered for two hardboiled eggs. She placed them in a boiling pot and went upstairs. When she came back, she took my temperature and wrote it down.

After a quick dinner of eggs and crackers, as the children said good night, the phone rang. It was the NYU doctor. She apologized for not making the earlier time, being busy with so many patients, and asked if I still wanted to talk. She had a soothing but authoritative voice. Though clearly knowledgeable, she lacked the healthcare professional's disposition of bullying the patient into silence with expertise. I described my symptoms to her and she agreed it sounded like COVID-19. She asked if I had been to the hospital to get tested and sounded genuinely relieved when I gave her the same long-winded, berating no with which the day before I had regaled my heart specialist's assistant. She told me it was best not to go. In addition to the hospitals being overwhelmed, there was the danger of something called *viral overload*. This is the possibility that an already infected person can make their condition worse by being exposed to more of the same virus. She feared this was happening all over the city with people lining up outside hospitals to get tested. The doctor's final inquiry took me to the refrigerator to consult with the different dates, times, and temperature readings Annabel had written on a large Post-it note. My most recent temperature had been 102. The highest I could see on the list had been 103 degrees, taken the previous morning. Dr. Patel said, "Great! It seems the fever has broken. You probably will start feeling better soon." I was taken aback. I hadn't felt much better that Thursday than during any of the previous two days. But her calm demeanor quieted my despair.

§

I awoke on Friday morning with a hankering for pound cake and *malta*. The combination was all my body wanted. But I couldn't get anything. Annabel was already downstairs helping the kids with school. Instead of feeling sorry for myself, I laid in bed peacefully, listening to the Russell

Brand podcast. The British comedian, turned Marxist revolutionary, turned podcaster with a spiritual bent, had an overexcited Dutch guest who complained about the medical establishment being too arrogant to promote the studies that had been done on his method. I learned later the man's name was Wim Hof, an extreme athlete who engaged in high altitude mountain climbing and snow runs bare chested and barefoot with nothing but cutoff shorts to protect him from the elements. Being left with four kids upon the suicide death of his wife in 1995, Mr. Hof found himself with severe depression. He concocted a series of breath-withholding meditations and exercises known as the Wim Hof method, which he now conveniently sold in app format. He railed against the medical establishment for not promoting the immunity boosting benefits of his breathing exercises. He was at worst a lovable charlatan. Towards the end of the podcast, I gingerly opened the window and sat cross-legged on the floor. To my surprise, my eyes welcomed *the light*. The COVID-induced reaction against it had vanished. The brightness of that spring morning felt soothing as Mr. Hof led Mr. Brand and his listeners through a breathing meditation.

As I inhaled "foooohly in" and exhaled "foooohly out," images of my wife and children came to mind. I recalled watching Jack and Conrad's attentive smiles the night before as they focused away from the grayness outside to the colorful world of *SpongeBob SquarePants*. I missed

51

watching the show with them. With a rush of exhilaration, I looked forward to once again being their designated goalie when they played soccer in the yard as the weather got warmer. I thought of Annabel and how much of a trooper she had been, working, taking care of our two boys, shopping, and bearing my neediness as she negotiated her own mild fever with calmed aplomb. I felt lucky. I realized I was getting better. I suspected, however, my appointed heart procedure, less than a week away, would be cancelled because I would be deemed too weak to go through with it. I would have to live with uncertainty.

§

I am not sure if I have fully recovered from COVID-19. I had antibodies. I donated plasma twice in the fall of 2020. But since March of that year, I haven't gone for more than two weeks straight without some strange ache or pain in some area of my body persisting for weeks. I haven't gotten the defibrillator implant yet. I live within the fragility of my body, breathing "foooohly in" and "foooohly out" every morning, and meditating every night. I don't expect any miraculous return to the vigor that underpinned my initial incredulity about the pandemic. I just try to enjoy each new break of daylight with my family.

There Will Be Blood

Eric Roberson

Henderson, Nevada, USA

It was one of those typical quarantine shut-down days. My mind drifted from the television pilot I'd been trying to write and getting nowhere with. I really needed to get some quality words on the page, and well, it just wasn't happening. My fingers were less on the keyboard and more on my phone. Scroll, scroll, scrolling the day away. Seconds turned to minutes, minutes turned to—I'm ashamed to admit: I flipped my way through the entirety of the Facebook universe, and I was no smarter for it. Just more bored, and a little disgusted at myself if I'm being honest. I slammed my phone down and away from me as if it had committed some awful sin.

I thought, *Man, you need to get yourself together. Do at least ONE thing productive today.*

I walked into the kitchen and inventoried what was needed for dinner. *What day is it?* I thought. I honestly didn't know. A mental yawn crept over my brain as I checked my watch. It told me the weather, my current heartrate, total steps taken, and calories burned. All of my rings were almost closed. My watch also told me it was Tuesday. I knew precisely what my mission was. Secure supplies for Taco Tuesday. No need for a grocery list. I knew exactly what to get, and a quick trip to the grocery store would get me back on track to being a productive writer again, right?

I'm a rule follower. I've spent more than half my existence in service of my country and community as a veteran and a cop. Rules, within reason, are there for a reason. With the things I've been exposed to, and the places I've been, I'm likely immune to most everything. I've been immunized for things I'll never be able to spell or pronounce, and I've exchanged body fluids with the best of them. I've been bled on, pooped on, peed on, and puked on many times. (This virus isn't going to kill me; it's going to be that damn TV pilot I'm trying to write.)

If the sign says *Wear a Mask,* that's what I'll do. If it says, *One Way Only* down the grocery aisles with those little arrows showing the way, I'll follow them. You see—it's not the wearing of a mask or the restrictions that bothered me. It was the foreboding cloud of panic and fear that seemed to hang over everyone and made normally nice people on edge. Including me.

I'm not big on crowds. COVID didn't bring this on; PTSD did. There was also something a bit unnerving to me about not being able to see people's faces anymore. I missed that human connection. I had been working on this fear, and I was up for the challenge. I knew what I had to do and exactly where everything was.

So, I wrapped my face and set out. I grabbed a sanitized cart and headed the *right way* down the aisle to my first stop. My cart was wounded. One of its wheels flopped about with every rotation making it list starboard and sound like a wash pan band marching down the aisle. It was also a little difficult to keep straight, but I didn't care much because I wouldn't be long.

In the butcher section I grabbed a pound of ground beef and was about to place it in the cart when I stopped. I remembered I was in a pandemic and needed to eat healthier. I put the ground beef back and opted for the ground turkey instead. I also remembered that Max, the bushy red-headed giant of a sixteen-year-old-son who hibernated in one of our back bedrooms, would need to eat after his workout. I did some quick math in my head.

Let's see, he's good for at least seventeen tacos, maybe more—I checked the calorie and exercise rings on my watch. *And if I can get these stupid rings closed, I'm good for two... or six. Maybe seven.*

I threw three pounds of ground turkey in the cart and wobbled it over to the tacos shells and seasoning. My glasses started fogging just like they did every time I had a mask on (or did math). I was making such good time I stopped by the dog food aisle and grabbed a few cans for the hound. I exited that aisle and decided since the water aisle was the next one over, and well...pandemic, I should grab extra.

Then the cart's right front wheel started locking up about every fourth rotation making it harder to push and keep straight. I was past the point of no return, but this cart wasn't making things easy. In the next aisle I grabbed two five-gallon water jugs, one in each hand, and placed them under the cart.

As I was placing the jugs under the cart, I scratched—more like cut—my left thumb on loose hanging hardware. I didn't remember feeling the injury at all. In fact, I only noticed when I started pushing the cart again and saw BRIGHT RED BLOOD lazily leaking out of my thumb. Not a big deal under normal circumstances. But no circumstance had been normal in a public place since March 2020.

Now the blood was snaking its way down the knuckle of my thumb and overtaking the nail. It showed no signs of slowing down either. So, just like I'd done a thousand times before March 2020, with a thousand other superficial wounds, I went to lick it, thinking that if I just cleaned up the sight of the blood I wouldn't risk having a HAZMAT crew tackle me in the aisle and hold me down while I was de-contaminated. But...yep, you remembered: I have a mask on, and I'm one of those patriotic types. So, now I've got old glory strapped to my face with a streak of blood smeared across it, and my glasses are fogged to the point I can't see anything.

I remembered the sanitation stations placed at the end of each aisle. The closest one was behind me at the end of the water aisle. Shielding my lacerated thumb the best I could from public view, I coaxed the cart around, nearly knocking over displays in the process and came face to face with another customer. She was riding in one of those scooters with the basket on the end of it and took up over half the aisle. She had on a giant plastic scuba helmet or fish bowl (I couldn't tell which in my haste) and had a voice somewhere between my fourth-grade teacher and my senior drill instructor from Parris Island from over 30 years ago.

"Can't read can you?" she scowled at me from behind her giant face-shield.

I said nothing.

We locked eyes.

Her eyes narrowed into little laser beams.

I noticed the sweat beading on her upper lip, and I wished like hell she was wearing a cloth mask. She was getting more and more red by the second, like I had double-parked a tractor trailer blocking her driveway. She wasn't going to budge an inch, and there was no way I was going to try to swing this jalopy of a cart back around.

In my head I could hear her thinking, *Is he really trying to go around me, against the arrows?* And this is where I found light in the COVID darkness. I smiled under my mask. I'd never ever done that. In fact, pre-pandemic, I rarely smiled at strangers. I smiled under my mask because I wondered how she would react if I took my bloody thumb and smeared the sign of the cross right in the middle of her face-shield while quoting lines from *The Exorcist,* "The power of Christ compels you..."

Of course, I didn't smear a bloody cross on her face-shield while quoting a horror movie. I wanted to eat tacos with Max. Instead, I squeezed past her ever so slowly with my broken cart full of turkey taco supplies, shielding my splayed thumb from view, all the while cheesing under my bloody American flag mask. Once past her, I almost started laughing until I reached the sanitation station and doused my blood-soaked thumb in a disinfecting wipe that made the pain choir in my head sing and my eyes water (no, I wasn't crying).

Thinking back, I smiled at the lady in the aisle because I knew she was going through something.

Just like I was.

Just like everybody is.

I'm sad it took a pandemic for me to learn that.

I'm working on it.

I'm also working on smiling outside that damn mask more often. I made it out of the store without any other incidents. I couldn't see through the fog enough to notice if anyone saw my thumb or my blood-streaked mask. If they did, I hope they smiled.

P.S. I finished that TV pilot, and I'm working on another one :)

Legacy Hand

James Roderick Burns

Edinburgh, Scotland, United Kingdom

> Rebinding and loss of leaves, especially of fly-leaves,
> have carried off names of owners and library-marks,
> and apart from that there are but few cases in which
> we are warranted in proclaiming from the aspect and
> character of the script that a book was written at one
> particular place and nowhere else.
> — MR James, *The Wanderings and Homes of
> Manuscripts*

L ooking back, from the month before it would be a
year since everything started, was a curious,
doubling experience. It couldn't possibly be a year.
Years were where lives took place, where careers were built
and marriages forged, or floundered; where babies became
toddlers and children unfurled the small coloured flags of
their personalities. No, it was a week. A longish week, no
question—perhaps the longest—and marked by
considerable stresses and strains, but surely no more than
that.

On the other hand, when I woke and settled into the
armchair, switched on my laptop and took my pills with a
mug of coffee, the view of the Edwardian flats across the
way shifting from sun-picked chimneys to rain-slicked slate,

even snow now and again, I felt this was the only life I had ever lived, and the years were simply marks on a tally stick, tiny components of some grander, permanent environment, and fleeting as dust-motes in a shaft of winter light.

I grunted, ordered another coffee on the delivery app.

I wondered which side would claim victory in today's office arms-race. E-mail was quick out of the gate. At the height of things in March—or was it February? August?—it was no contest: three or four hundred over an eight-hour span meant no more than a minute to read and respond to each, with the next slamming into the bunker the instant I returned fire. Small white bullets, rifled with exclamation marks. Larger ordnance dropping with the weight and whistle of doodlebugs.[1] But nothing waited for me, save perhaps the insistent bell of the day's first video-conference.

Now Teams was coming on strong, stubbing out a last cigarette and rolling up its sleeves for the fight.

In between puffs of gun smoke, I waited for that small blue singing box in the corner of the screen; the torturous grind of its start-up routine; my hand looming, fish-white, in the camera's eye to adjust the angle of the screen before I settled alongside the others in their Hollywood squares. Some chose a neutral background, the ultra-modern white

---

[1] The buzzing sound of the German V-1 bombs dropped on London during World War II prompted Londoners to call them *buzz bombs* and *doodlebugs* (flying insects).

box, stripped of personality, others a futuristic beach, Scottish glen or the reaching span of an abstract bridge. I blurred my background so no one could see the laundry, or my daughter sneaking by on her way to the kitchen.

I imagine the Speaking Hand feature was designed to let the chair control an unruly babble—impose order on overlapping ripples of voices keen to make a point, or simply register their presence. But every time, clicking that icon— fingers spread wide in menacing outline—I was catapulted back to primary school: *Please, sir! I know—I know!* Or, in darker moods, thrust back into the limelight of incompetence, forced by the great pedagogical digit to warble painfully on the recorder, stagger through a gassy quagmire of sums.

Now I spent my days endlessly pressing and releasing the little hand.

I watched as the bank of screens flipped from one chair to another, spectacles peering into the lens for the next agenda item, recognising a colleague, asking—with rapidly-souring humour—'Is that a legacy hand? Did you have another point to make?'

I could always make a further point—and one more, then another, and another—but it remained a legacy hand, nonetheless.

On the good days (when my daughter was engaged with school, my wife with the latest assault on American democracy) I approached the whole draining, never-ending

61

battlefield with a slightly mellower eye. On other days, I felt like a bundle of skin and bones being dropped into a meat-grinder one message at a time.

'It can't be so bad,' my colleagues in other organisations said—'surely things have slowed down, now we're on top of it?' Perhaps they were right. They talked of children or pets, held up the fuzzy little blighters to the camera for comic relief, laughed when a dog picked up another's digital *woof* and relayed it around the country in one looping, continuous bark.

I remember a night not so long ago when I was awake at midnight, the unlit park opposite the flat black with snow, the city knocked silent at the close of another day. My daughter walked in and threw open a window, pulled the board out from under my laptop and stuck it into the storm.

'Look!' she said.

On the scratched surface of the wood, snowflakes lit and melted. She held a hand towards the cone of light from a nearby street-lamp. The snow was falling slant-wise through its beam, and for a moment we tracked the passage of individual flakes down towards the pavement, their motion slowing in the observation, as though the act of looking brought poise and significance to an otherwise galloping, meaningless headlong jumble.

She turned back to the room.

'You want to go out?' my daughter said.

I groaned. A nine-hour day done, with dinner and

washing-up, then much the same tomorrow. But under the cone, the rate of snowfall seemed to be lessening, each flake turning more purposefully towards the window, as if in invitation. I did a rapid inventory of hats, coats and gloves, then nodded.

'Alright, then.'

The blizzard had tailed off to a light, occasional dusting, then nothing but frigid black air when we made it downstairs. Where the cobbles had been was a long white knitted scarf wrapped around the junction, its surface knobbly and perfect as a Shetland jumper. The spiny branches of the trees overhanging the park were caked with a thick layer of icing, and in the children's play area the bucket-rides and climbing frames were furry with snow-deposits, lying slumped and mysterious as items long-forgotten in the dustiest attic. No one had ventured out. All the paths wound away blank and empty, stretching plump with potential around silent corners. We stood for a moment in the dark, cold nothing, and smiled.

By now everyone was used to the spectacle of empty streets, parks with a single lugubrious dog wandering round on his lonesome, the only real action a nightly emptying of the recycling bins by a clanking, flashing lorry, hydraulics screeching like pterodactyls in the darkness, but now the emptiness was new and complete, somehow soothing.

My daughter walked down a row of cars, dipping a glove into the thick mounds on the bonnets, kicking out lines on the kerb, drawing love hearts on windscreens. I stood for a minute doing nothing at all. Then, as though at some unheard, secret alarm the streets began to fill with people: first a young couple in their twenties, with thin sweatshirts and granny-bobbled hats, untroubled by the freeze; an older man knocking flakes from his flat cap; a young mother with two children in tow, holding hands like ornaments draped around a Christmas tree.

I smiled; my daughter laughed. We moved apart automatically to the required distance, began walking down the road. The snow creaked underfoot and soaked up the sound. I found a drain mysteriously clean, steam curling through its shocking brown bars. She penguined down a side street, marking the fresh white page with splayed sneakers, stooping now and again for a handful of snow. Each time she approached, grinning with clasped hands, I dodged away and we laughed again.

Down the main road, round the block and back to the park. In our brief absence half the city seemed to have crept out into the night. The children were still there, their mother bent over a low wall, forming armouries of snowballs. The boy—all of four years old—crept up to his sister with a glistening icy bullet.

'Ha!'

It missed by a country mile. The girl grabbed one of the snowballs and lobbed it high, straight over her brother's head. It sailed through his outstretched fingers, thwacking into a street sign with a reverberating *bong*, and stuck there like a mound of putty.

When we got back inside it was late but I made coffee and hot chocolate anyway, and we sat for a while before my daughter took herself off to bed. I lingered, steam dwindling from my cup, looking from the closed silver laptop to the blank square of window, back again. I rubbed the grease from my phone screen and checked the time. Not long till I'd need to be in, and on again. In the dead quiet of morning I could hear artillery beginning to rattle in the magazine, the doodlebugs settling in their frames for the first of the day's bombing runs.

Looking back, from the month before it would be a year since everything started, was a curious, doubling experience. The hand was waiting—it never really went down—but for a moment, I felt the high sizzling thrill of a snowball passing through fingers, on the way to who-knew-where, but for that instant absolutely free, and tapped the laptop with my knuckles, and drained my coffee, and went to bed.

What Year Is It?

Margot Douaihy

Northampton, Massachusetts, USA

my niece asks,
like a tiny time-traveler. *2020*, I say.
Still? No school, no playground.
In town, she waves to kids in masks,
friends she hasn't seen in months.
When the sickness is over, she forecasts,
everyone will sing, like in The Grinch.
Spelling JUSTICE for our protest sign,
I try to smile with the *i* sound.
Later, I turn her upside down
so she can watch trees flying.
The grass is in the sky! she cries.
How rare it is to let ourselves
be scared, to hold someone
as the world changes,
even for a second.

The Other Virus

Ivana Cvejic

Las Vegas, Nevada, United States

Entrepreneur—it's not a skill or a job; it's a passion. As a passion I suppose it's similar to being a parent; there's never any question of giving up. True entrepreneurs always put their businesses and employees ahead of their own needs because their businesses are like their children. On the downside, they get into the habit of trying to control everything because they worry and want to protect their children while allowing them to succeed and to flourish.

I've started three companies in my career thus far. The first two were consulting companies and only required the expertise I had developed in my many years as a recruiter; starting these companies proved to be a natural transition. The third was a software company I started with my friend, and as it turned out, I didn't know what I was getting myself into...

As with any new venture, whether personal or business-related, we had a great vision inspired by the extensive experience between us. Our different backgrounds were a perfect compliment to one another, and we had a combined skillset that covered every area important to build and grow a successful software company. Our goals were completely aligned, but there were so many things we didn't take into account that created obstacles for us later on. Starting this company required so much more upfront capital than we had planned for due to timelines extending unexpectedly (a very normal scenario for a software startup that we weren't aware of), so much detailed planning, and an incredible balance between the technical and the creative.

We may not have understood the resources we'd need since we had never built a software company before, but having been brought up by immigrant parents, we definitely knew what it meant to sacrifice luxuries in order to build something sustainable. We also knew how passionate we both were about building something we could call our own.

Our original vision for the company was based on two basic principles:

1. Build the best product on the market and
2. create the type of culture we never got to be a part of during our corporate careers.

For the product, we focused on the pain points we personally felt while running large teams during our corporate positions: there was no good software on the market to help enterprise companies manage their recruiting efforts and metrics associated with their workforce. Corporate waste has always been a big pet peeve of mine; I saw it throughout my corporate career, and I became an expert at identifying it, restructuring teams and processes, then renegotiating vendor contracts so each business unit was utilizing their resources in the most efficient way possible while hiring the best talent. My partner knew technology inside and out and was confident she could build a product that would be easy to use and accomplish all of the goals we knew were important for every company. Her ability to develop complex solutions for large companies by looking at the problem and reverse-engineering it to find the right solution was a rare talent, and even though I didn't have any knowledge of the software world, I knew she could do it.

For two people to handle everything a company needs to begin and grow is no easy feat, but we powered through, allowing our excitement and passion to carry us after sleepless weeks, and in the first two years we had a shiny new product to sell and a ripe market ready to listen. For two entrepreneurs with no children, we truly took on this task as if it were our first child. We only thought of that child, giving it all of our time and attention and not once considering that we could give it up, regardless of the fatigue.

Through our next several growth stages everything was looking great on the outside. The customers we brought on were recognized throughout the country, propelling us into even greater interest from others, and our name was becoming recognized in our industry. Our team had grown substantially, and we had built processes that now looked like a sustainable operation, not a startup anymore.

With all of our successes, however, there came a muted

but distinct feeling of dissatisfaction. It was quite small at first but grew within me without any conscious realization. I can't even say when it started, for it was truly a tiny leakage difficult to detect but over time was seeping out optimism and creativity.

Then COVID hit.

After the initial shock of COVID-19 and the realization across the world that we could no longer conduct ourselves or our businesses in the same fashion, after the fear and anxiety settled into some knowledge of what was happening around us and we realized this wasn't going away any time soon, the light began to shine on the darkness I had created. It was faint at first, a small glow infiltrating the outer layer of the defense I had built over time that was now weakening. "Why am I killing myself when everything just goes up in dust?" "What's the point?" Those thoughts permitted a small light to penetrate the cracks in the armor, just enough to show me that letting go of some control was loosening me up for new ideas, and the shutdown wasn't the end of the world. There were some opportunities that appeared to me as the armor fell away, and I realized I could use this downtime as an opportunity to pivot. "I might as well start taking care of myself while I have time," I told myself, and that's when my eyes and heart started opening up to a much brighter reality.

I began to realize that despite my ideals (or lofty goals),

Pre-COVID was about closing deals and working with people who were also obsessed with closing the next deal, turning my beautiful child into a monster of greed and desperation that was slowly eating away at my company and taking over. The ever-present fear of missing our next goal, which would perpetuate an unbalance in our spending plan is just one example of so many things that perpetuated my anxiety. This anxiety manifested in a short temper with very little patience for training and coaching others, which I had always loved to do and was one of the reasons we wanted to create a culture of collaboration. Every delay I faced turned into a blaming game with questions about why the team couldn't work faster, questions about their motivations even, to the point where I would feel the hesitation on the other end of the phone because they were afraid of "pissing me off." I've never been a fan of the blame game; it was one of the main reasons I left the corporate world so many years ago, and here I was curating the best blame game I could muster, no assistance necessary.

One particular example, a collaboration between one of our partners and one of the largest consumer companies in the country, began as a mutually respectful and exciting project of creativity and problem-solving. The fact that we landed such a large customer was surreal at such an early stage of our company, and we put all of our resources into making them happy and developing features for them that would help automate their daily work. About a year in, senior leadership with our partner changed and the culture with it. The demands our partner made on us for additional resources while asking for discounts, shrouded in not-so-subtle threats, made working with this partner less and less appealing and more like a chore, but the end client we both supported had such an enticing brand it was difficult to break away from the opportunity. Each one of our employees who supported our partner detested the task, and the spirit of our environment started to sag with the heaviness of a child who was constantly beaten down by its parent, bullied to submission every day, rarely given a treat or any other type of relief. This heaviness permeated into every crevice of our company, and because we were still small at the time and feared the loss of revenue, we kept going because we just assumed we had to. And we did. We still had some priorities straight and felt an obligation to our employees, not to mention the immense amount of time it took to properly train them, so we sucked it up and continued to allow a foreign entity in the guise of our partner to suck the energy right out of us. Hatred and resentment of the people I chose to do business with was the beginning of a life and company I would never have chosen for myself or for my trusted employees. Then awareness and change was forced upon us.

COVID brought to light some of the darkness that had ensued inside of my business while I was trying to control all. That control, that "parents' protective nature," was strangling me and my business. The good intent turned into a metaphorical virus that spread into fear, anxiety, sleeplessness, and then mutated into something I've seen in other entrepreneurs and company cultures and swore I would never allow for myself. It turned me against myself, losing my sense of instinct and going for the money instead of the experience and passion, which I know from previous experience never turns out well. In being forced to recognize that I couldn't control everything, I started to relax enough to recognize the truth of the fear-virus that had started to infiltrate my entire life, and through that recognition I started to actually listen. I made an important decision about two weeks into lock-down: I had absolutely no control over the business situation created by the pandemic, and I couldn't just sit still and watch as the world and my company collapsed, so I went to work on bringing back the authenticity of my soul and the soul of my company. My inner self was the only thing that I could take some control over and change for the better.

I started with a gratitude book. Every day I wrote down what I was grateful for before I went to bed at night. This small exercise that took all of three minutes opened up my emotional memory and reminded me of all the blessings I had and the immense amount of support I had collected through my years of building relationships with family, mentors, and a wonderful team. The next step was meditation, which taught me how to be present. In that presence there were profound lessons of who I am, where I came from, and why I was a successful executive in the first place. My resume had some impressive experiences and recognizable names on it, but it was my natural intuitive nature, life experiences, and support system I'd built of intelligent and loving people around me that constructed this amazing human being who was willing to take risks and put herself in harm's way to create something unique.

In just a few short days of being present my whole being vibrated with the remarkable knowledge that if this company failed, I did not. I turned my day-to day drive for more revenue into working from the inside out: I worked on communicating with my team in a way that showed great promise even as the world around us was collapsing; I helped my team manage their fears by example: changing my fear to enthusiasm for something exciting, unknown, and opportunistic for future possibilities. That energy started to resonate and spread to others.

When we finally lost our largest customer, about five months into the shutdown, I was prepared. The feeling of relief and calm, while not surprising, was a welcoming and interesting feeling that gave me courage to have stronger conversations with other customers. My negotiation skills became sharper because I was now working without fear. My inner voice was constantly telling me "our product is worth more; they know it, and if they don't, then I don't want to do business with them." I was in no financial position to be turning business away, but I felt liberated and somehow knew that the right business would come with this new-found strength.

A few weeks into my "inner" work, I noticed my conversations with employees became less controlling and more forgiving, and my interactions with those I was doing business with was more authentic. The passionate entrepreneur who started a company based on the desire to build something meaningful, to cultivate jobs and a great culture for talented professionals was breathing again. Providing a sustainable product for business professionals around the world that alleviated administration so they can get back to having conversations again........that entrepreneur was coming back to life.

When COVID hit, the actual virus was putting people in mass graves and spreading fear amongst world populations. The personal "fear-virus" I had manufactured unconsciously forced me to finally recognize what was right in front of me. Everything halted, as we confronted an epic global event that nobody knew how to address. But while governments, hospitals, and pharma worked around the clock to find medical solutions to protect us all, the virus was also acting as a healing tool individually, slowing me down for a hot minute, bringing to light the obvious: I cannot control everything, and I need to lean on others to create solutions. While my revelation and good fortune to recognize the silver lining to this pandemic was in direct contrast to the mania happening around me, the extreme gratitude I felt contributed to the compassion I was able to extend to others, which perpetuated a positive cycle of healing for myself and my business.

This "personal" virus that almost killed me was killed off by an actual virus that affected millions of people around the world. Without the big pause that COVID forced upon me I'm not sure what I would have turned into or if I would have recognized the poison I had allowed to seep into my daily life and business, but I'm grateful to the difficult lockdown period for giving me back my life, my passion, and my authentic self. While we're all deeply saddened by the deaths this virus caused, we also have a new outlook on how to move forward. I don't waste my time anymore on people who could potentially bring poison into my business, and I've now started to attract the type of partners I enjoy working with. As a result, my whole being and my business are thriving with new customers we enjoy working with, and my desire to continue building great products is back with gusto. I wake up every day thankful for the lessons this last year has brought. I continue to work on expanding on those lessons and try to remember that by loosening my grip on the outcome and focusing on the task in the present moment, I will accomplish everything I set out to do eight years ago.

I sincerely hope my story will inspire other business owners to look within and be grateful and proud of everything they've built. We are the heart of the American economy and have it within our power to cultivate a culture of creativity and collaboration every single day. Let's support one another and embrace change together.

Alb Albi

Laura Valdez-Pagliaro

Maadi, Cairo, Egypt

Šukran

Egypt is the third Arabic speaking country my family and I moved to in eleven years but the first where not knowing common phrases was sometimes an obstacle. When career options transferred us from the US to Kuwait—then Dubai, then elsewhere, then Kuwait again—I was eager to learn my host country's language. Everywhere I went, though, someone spoke English and Arabic and at least one other language, making daily life easy enough that my urgency to learn Arabic evaporated. If before moving to Cairo I had dedicated as much time to learning common phrases as to wishing I could speak and read Arabic, I might have arrived more self-sufficient, not having to rely on the lifelines saved on my phone to translate for me.

Despite how much simpler daily life in Cairo would have been with a cache of phrases, I have taken only two Arabic lessons. Both were in Kuwait, and both alongside my husband, who is a natural at picking up languages. By chance or some miraculous intervention, several years before our unexpected move to the Arabian Gulf, his ease with languages inspired me to give him what turned out to be a prescient birthday surprise: Arabic courses at the

Middle East Institute in Washington, D.C. During our first lesson, he impressed our teacher—an expat himself and coincidentally Egyptian—with his mastery of colloquialisms and the fundamentals of MSA, Modern Standard Arabic. Going into our first lesson, I could say "thank you," *šukran.* Having been raised by a woman who, even at her lowest moments, expressed gratitude effusively with a hand-over-heart thank you and soft sideways head tilt, I cling to *šukran.*

The pragmatic reason I discontinued private lessons was that managing my routines did not require Arabic, while the defeating reason I stopped was the homework: memorize the alphabet. The Middle East Institute guided my husband through six weeks of learning the Arabic alphabet. Our Egyptian teacher in Kuwait me gave me 48 hours. It was an impossible task that left me discouraged. At the end of the lesson, I could just get past '*alif* and *bä* but had trouble discerning the calligraphy and sound of the third letter of the alphabet, *ta',* and the fourth, also *ta'* but with three not two dots above it. So I said to my teacher, "*la šukran,*" no thank you. Since then, the exigencies of settling into Cairo in the middle of a pandemic and selective introversion stopped me from signing up for Arabic. Eventually I might finally take suitably paced lessons at a community center expats frequent, *inšalla,* God willing. In the meantime, I collect practical Egyptian Arabic listening to conversations happening around me and repeating what I hear, and watching Arabic language films on Netflix, most of them filmed in Egypt, some in my new neighborhood.

Kullu tamām? It's all good!
Mid-May, 2020, we said conflicted, heartbroken goodbyes to a fully shut down Kuwait. From an eerily empty airport terminal we boarded one of two out-going flights that had resumed daily departures since COVID closed borders, with a highly restricted number of passengers and a crew in white, full-body protective coveralls. We spent a socially-distanced summer at our stateside home under my favorite sky in the west Texas border city where I was born and raised. In July, we celebrated our younger son's milestone 10th birthday in COVID fashion, with cake and close family spread out on our back lawn. In August, after a 28-hour layover in a drearily wet, deserted NYC, we boarded an EgyptAir flight with too few empty seats and too many unmasked faces. Ten hours after takeoff, as we began our descent into Cairo, we flew over the rising limestone pyramids of Kings Khufu, Khafre, and Menkaure guarded by the Great Sphynx on the Giza Plateau. From my center aisle seat, Cairo looked just like the sprawling ancient-urbanized time capsule I imagined but had not foreseen as a stop on our expat journey. Moving to Cairo during the pandemic summed up what living abroad has been so far, a series of unexpected departures and nervous arrivals without precedent. Uncertain but *tamām*, good.

Kullu tamām, meaning "everything is good," was the first full phrase I distinctly discerned in Cairo. It was a breakthrough moment, being able to pluck *kullu tamām* out of conversations in which I was completely sidelined. Learning its meaning from one of my lifelines, *kullu tamām* felt reassuring. Depending on intonation, sometimes *kullu tamām* asks a question, sometimes it answers the same question, sometimes it confirms an answer. The first time I said *kullu tamām* out loud was when the produce vendor at a neighborhood market, Mr. Kamal, a gentleman with the formal grace I have come to associate with Arab culture, who warmly greets and thanks me in English with the phrase "you are most welcome," asked with some circumspection, *tamām*? Yes, *kullu tamām*, I answered automatically, naturally, although not truthfully, like my mother would have when very little felt good, and *šukran*, like she taught me. In one word, Mr. Kamal asked two questions: Do you have all you need, and is everything OK? Taking from his extended arms the Italian parsley and Egyptian Baladi lemons he chose with deliberate attention, I felt embraced in Arabic by Mr. Kamal's *tamām*, and as if Maadi, our corner of Cairo, were starting to become a part of me and I of it.

Maadi is a neighborhood of Cairo on the Nile with a glamourous history evoked in a blend of traditional Arab and European Colonial architecture, embassies and large villas guarded by private armed security detail, varieties of crawling bougainvillea always in bloom, and wide trees whose tangled branches arch into canopies and swallow streetlights. Because we arrived during the pandemic, we only know COVID Cairo. By accounts from expats who were here before the coronavirus, some since before the revolution of 2011, pre-COVID Cairo, Maadi especially, was sophisticated and dynamic, the international school (800 meters from our apartment), where we send our two boys, a hub of socializing and endless activities. I lack pre-COVID Cairo expats' frame of reference, but to me it seems the virus merely tempered Maadi's pre-pandemic vibe. Coronavirus never fully shut Maadi down for long, or came close to shaking its confidence.

In the one square kilometer of Maadi we've settled into, the shadow of the pandemic floats over our bubble of comfort and security among poverty and hardship. Masks are mandatory in public spaces, so almost everyone has one, if not covering the mouth and nose, then on the chin, around the elbow or wrist, or tucked in a pocket. Gently enforced curfews close cafes and restaurants earlier than usual, but not completely. Streets and the squares they intersect are never deserted. Social distancing is more a suggestion than a mandate, except at the boys' school, where strictly enforced mitigation protocol allowed face-to-face learning throughout the academic year and steadily kept the school community COVID rate impressively below 1%.

Beyond the international school's high campus walls, rising COVID numbers reported by the Ministry of Health & Population shut down local schools and yet seemed perplexingly low for a country with a population its size. To the Egyptians in our immediate circle, however, the numbers made sense. Since COVID-19 statistics rely on reporting, cases among those who do not have access or choose not to seek care at a hospital or clinic are not counted, their contacts impossible to trace. The official numbers, then, present data that tell one collective story while the lived experiences of those who have gotten sick and recovered but never tested for the virus, and those who lost someone over the year from what might have been the virus though they will never know for sure, tell more.

Ilḥamdu lillāh

The discrepancy between official coronavirus numbers versus experiences dictating personal choices strikes me as neatly analogous to the use of MSA taught by most Arabic teachers and used mainly by academics, journalists, and government leaders, versus the cultural diversity expressed in colloquial Arabic taught by mothers and fathers and used daily by everyone. COVID-19 statistics and precautions from the government are relevant in our bubble the way that MSA conventions and their dictates are to native Arabic speakers: generally applicable but not strict enough to be adhered to other than when the right occasion calls. "No" and "yes" illustrate the point. In both MSA and colloquial Arabic, no is *la*, like the sixth syllable on the C major scale. "Yes" in Classical Arabic (the language of the Quran) is *ajal* and *na'am*. Native speakers and students of Arabic are taught *la* and *na'am* formally, but my ears rarely pick up *na'am*. In Levantine dialects I heard spoken in Kuwait by Arabs from Lebanon, Syria, Jordan, and Palestine, "yes" is *ah*. Among Lebanese and Syrians, "yes" is also *eh*. *Aaha* is another Arabic affirmative vocalization like um-hmm in U.S. English. In Egyptian Arabic, *aywa* is "yes." Whichever the dialect, if asked, "How do you say 'yes' in Arabic," a native speaker will likely give the same answer they were formally taught, *na'am*. But in other contexts, the colloquial "yes" Arabic speakers choose has the potential to do more than affirm. It may reveal cultural and national origin.

The polite inquiry "how are you?" may also convey cultural and national specificity. The MSA way to ask is *keif halāk*. *Keif halāk* is the phrase formally taught but infrequently used among friends and family. The colloquial contraction of "how are you?" in Arabic dialects is *kīfak* (m.), *kīfik* (f.), and *kifkun* (pl.). The answer to all forms of *keif halāk*, however, is *ilḥamdu lillāh*. "Praise God" or "thank God." Religious or not, Muslim or not, *ilḥamdu lillāh* is the response to all variations of "how are you?" too, including how have you been, how is your family, how did exams go for your children, how are you feeling, are you better, have you recovered, and how are you coping? When

I hear *ilɧamdu lillāh* I'm momentarily transported home to the US/Mexico border, to my mother and her sweet *tías* who raised her and taught her to answer "how are you" with *gracias a Dios*. I hear *ilɧamdu lillāh* daily and often, so too I hear mother in Arabic.

Yaḷḷa Beena

Five months after moving to Cairo, finding a personal trainer became imperative, overriding any inclination I had to finding an Arabic teacher. I have been running regularly for decades to keep my head clear and anxiety manageable. In the first few months after arriving, I was most at ease exploring Maadi on morning runs after sending the boys off to school. But I found myself losing my balance, I kept stumbling into fixed objects, barely catching myself. On my first run in Wadi Degla Protectorate, a natural reserve in the middle of Maadi, a loose stone on a wide, clear path took me down. That fall was less alarming than not having the strength or balance to do things around the house I'd had no problem doing before moving to Cairo, like swapping out 19-liter bottles in our water dispenser or lifting mattress corners when changing sheets. I needed to do more than run to stay physically and mentally well. I needed to regain the balance and strength I'd somehow lost in the move to Cairo.

Our older son needed more physical activity, too. The boys' school had phased in face-to-face instruction but continued to suspend on-campus sports and activities because of COVID. My son's personal goals were to develop boxing skills and build up his lean frame, but I knew he was struggling to muscle his way emotionally through yet another move. He needed an outlet to relieve the pressure that comes with being transplanted in a new country. Again. Transferring to a new school. Again. Missing his old friends while finding his place among new ones. Again. To say nothing of the ordinary challenges of being a teenager navigating his first year in high school and the extraordinary ones the pandemic handed him. So in January we started training separately with Omda.

When we first met Omda, Egypt was moving beyond a second COVID peak. Numbers of new cases were falling. Officials attributed the decline to government restrictions and mandatory use of masks in public. Omda half-jokingly suspected the falling COVID cases in Cairo had more to do with local Egyptians' hearty constitutions, their immune systems fortified by the city's pollution, which tends to rank highest worldwide. When he is not training privately, Omda works at a popular gym that shut down temporarily at the onset of the pandemic. He never talked about the strain he experienced during the shutdown, but he always had a story to share about being lifted up when he most needed a miracle. Despite the health and financial risks, Omda was casually consistent about wearing a mask, but better about maintaining the recommended distance from clients, and steadfast when it came to having his friends' backs, settling

86

disputes among neighbors, intervening on behalf of strangers in danger, giving his clients more than we thought we needed.

Meeting Omda when we did feels like the same divine intervention that answered his prayers. Omda prays daily. He quoted the Quran to explain himself, his motivations, his life perspective. He was uncannily perceptive in a way that seemed celestially inspired. Omda was hulking, but he reminded me often of my petite mother who also leaned on prayer, tried earnestly to live by her Catholic faith, and whose intuition was extraordinary, sometimes intrusively so.

To motivate us, Omda barked an Arabic phrase I adopted from him, *yaḷḷa beena*. "Let's go!" When my son told him he wanted to learn to box, Omda boomed *yaḷḷa beena*, "you are a champion." Omda motivated my son to push beyond his self-imposed obstacles with humor and encouragement. In time, my son's physique started changing, and his *roh*, his soul, started healing. Training with Omda, he steadily grew less on edge and more comfortable in own skin, more at peace and ease, *ilḥamdu lillāh*.

Omda also tended to the emotional source of my physical imbalance while working relentlessly on my core. When I started training with Omda, no other set of reps made me viscerally crankier than sit-ups. On an especially vulnerable day, Omda witnessed my frustration stir a deep

87

sadness connected to my mother. After straining to sit up, I put my head on my knees and silently cried. When she was about my age, I was seven or so, my mom signed herself up for adult beginner swim lessons at the YWCA. She brought me with her because I was afraid to be left alone, and she had no one to stay with me. During her lesson, I stood watch on tiptoe at the door leading from the frigidly air-conditioned reception desk to the humid pool, looking out for her white bathing cap decorated with fern, magenta, and burnt sienna rubber daisies to appear and disappear past a square paned window partially clouded over. The heady smell of chlorine seemed to rise out of the concrete walls and cast a greenish-grey halo around the white lights suspended over the pool. From my side of the door, I felt my mother's desire to float on her own, along with our shared hope that she would, wane. In the locker room, at arm's length, I watched her bend her head forward and silently cry into her towel. Her wave of sadness frightened me, but I knew what was coming. She had reached the nadir of a seasonal swing that gripped her cyclically throughout the year, was at a place I had seen her so many times before that I had come to anticipate it, knowing she would likely stay weighed down for a while, present and unreachable.

" *Yalla beena*," Omda gently coaxed, COVID and Muslim Arab custom keeping him a meter away, "You have a good heart."

Ente ah-yooni

Some widely used Arabic terms of endearment spoken across Arab cultures reference the body. In Arabic, a beloved, be it a lover, dearest friend, parent, or child, may be called *nour 'yooni*, light of my eyes, or *ente ah-yooni*, my eyes, or eyes of my eyes, *'yoon 'yooni*, the doubling conveying deeper, more intensely felt love and affection. *Enta 'umri*, the title of a one-hour long love song by the legendary Oum Kulthum, is also common. The "i" at the end indicates possession and *'umr* literally means age, but the meaning of *enta 'umri* is closer to "my whole existence" or "my entire being." Other common expressions of love are *hayaat hayaati*, life of my life, *roh rohi*, soul of my soul, and *alb albi*, heart of my heart. Adding these to my treasure trove of Arabic phrases not only gave me more ways to express love but expanded my capacity to connect and to empathize with others in the community that made us feel, as Mr. Kamal, Omda, and Yasmin unfailingly did, most welcome.

Yasmin is an aide at my younger son's elementary school. She teaches little ones throughout the day. Every morning drop-off and afternoon pick-up during the first year back on campus after the pandemic moved learning online, she was at my younger son's assigned gate making sure kids' temperatures were checked and that they were reunited with their parent, sibling, driver, or nanny. She stylishly coordinated brightly colored masks with her tunic and *hijab*, and was unfailingly warm and welcoming, the Arab way. Yasmin was one of my lifelines, not to translate (though I knew she would be more than happy to) but to WhatsApp if I was running late and wanted my son reassured that I was on my way to him. At pick-up, I usually stood meters away from the gate, keeping a good distance from the masked clusters pressing forward who were less vigilant about COVID mitigation practices and more extroverted than me. Yasmin and I picked up the habit of making eye contact from a distance. We greeted each other silently, placing our right palms over our heart, a common gesture in Arab countries that can express many things depending on the situation: hello, thank you, I appreciate you.

One afternoon I arrived earlier for pick up than usual, wondering if I'd see Yasmin. She hadn't been at her post in weeks. I was worried she was among the faculty COVID cases reported by the school nurse. It was a relief to see her when security opened the gates, and out she walked into the sun, taking her usual place. Instead of greeting her from a distance I stepped close to Yasmin. She was well *ilḥamdu lillāh*, but a close contact had tested positive, she explained. Following COVID mitigation protocol, she was obliged to test negative and quarantine for ten days before returning to school. I asked about her family. "*Ilḥamdu lillāh*. My mom is well," she said reassuringly but with a dip in her voice that gave me pause. She read from the upper half of my face not covered by a mask that I was missing a part of her story. Remembering we were new to Cairo, she continued, "Last June, my father and I tested positive for COVID on the same day." Yasmine recovered. Her father did not. Less than one year later, the family was deeply mourning their loss. "I am so sorry," I managed to say, just as kids began lining up inside the gate behind her. Regaining awareness of where I was, I realized the sidewalk had grown crowded, ringing with parents, siblings, drivers, and nannies vying for Yasmin's attention.

Walking home with my son, I glanced at Yasmin's WhatsApp profile picture. What I had registered as a photo of Yasmin was actually Yasmin and her father superimposed on each other forming one perfectly aligned half of the other's face, a soft seam joining them from hairline to chin faintly perceptible. It was striking. Yasmin is as identical to her father as I to my mother. She has her father's oval face and warm smile. I have my mother's high cheekbones and silver-white hair. Transcendently, Yasmin's Photoshopped image flattened onto one plane the spatial distance between her and her father that I experience in relation to my mother when I look in the mirror and see both of us. I could feel Yasmin's loss of her father to COVID in a way I wouldn't have had words for had we not moved to Cairo. He was the eyes of her eyes, her *ente ah-yooni*.

Alb Albi

My year of COVID started a few months before Yasmin's on March 8, 2020. International Women's Day. The day my mother died. A woman who raised seven daughters, she could not have chosen a more fitting day to pass peacefully into the light that surely lit her way.

That Sunday morning, the nursing staff who had cared for her with grace and compassion, gathered quietly along the halls outside her room. I wonder what the weeks after her passing were like for them, how instead of staying a respectful distance they stood at the bedsides of their residents holding their hands in place of family and loved ones COVID kept away. Like the nurses and attendants who felt our loss, the morning sky seemed to want to honor my mom, too. It was raining. The mountains were misty. My mom loved the smell of the desert rain, and she loved the desert mountains.

COVID did not take my mom, but life had begun shutting down because of it. My husband, who stayed with our sons, was dreading imminent border closures. As if my mom orchestrated final acts of her love for me, I made it back to my family through Dubai on what turned out to be the last Emirates flight to Kuwait. Hours after departure Dubai shut down for several months. Finding myself neither stranded nor locked down alone, barely making it back to my husband and sons, was as miraculous as getting to my mom three weeks before when she was lucid, able to squeeze my hand, cup my cheek, stroke my hair, lay her right hand across her chest and tell me, "you have a good heart." *Šukran, alb albi.*

The Light Within

Kerri Younger

Barrow-in-Furness, Cumbria, United Kingdom

I gripped the steering wheel of my car as it sat stationary outside of my local supermarket, my breathing ragged, my knuckles white. I pushed my forehead, beaded with sweat, against the cool leather of the wheel. Squeezing my eyes closed, I tore away the mask that had been hanging loosely from one ear and threw it in the vague direction of the passenger seat. My body shook as a wracking sob broke free. A solitary tear worked its way clear of my tightly closed eyelid and glided its way down my nose.

I could hear my own heartbeat roaring in my ears, deafening me to everything else. It thumped its quickened timbre against the inside of my skull as I gasped for air. A tsunami of emotion threatening to engulf me, a slow, anguished wail escaping from me as I gulped hungrily for air.

Pushing myself away from the steering wheel, I used the back of my shaking hand to wipe away the tear now hanging from the tip of my nose. I sniffled back the threat of more tears, pushing my spine against the seat and arching my back to force me to look up at the ceiling of my car, whilst I steadied my breathing.

How many more of these anxiety attacks was I going to have to endure before there was any semblance of 'normal' again? When I wouldn't have to constantly think and worry about keeping my distance, making sure I wore my mask, and washing my hands until the skin was red raw and cracked? The maw of anxiety and fear opened wide and threatened to accept me into the dark abyss beyond.

With my breathing beginning to slow, and my heart no longer hammering in my chest, I lowered my head to stare out through the windscreen. I leant down to turn the key in the ignition and with the rev of the engine, pulled out of the parking space. I drove home in a foggy daze, pulling up outside the house, not wholly remembering the journey that had gotten me there.

After letting myself in, greeting the cat and giving her a scratch under her chin, I made myself a cup of sweetened tea and sat on the settee staring unblinkingly into nothingness. The message tone on my phone broke me from my daze. The screen revealed my friend Jess's name.

Hey lovely, how are you getting on? Xx, the message read.

I sighed, unlocked my phone and opened the message. I squinted as I tried to think about how I'd respond. Did she really want to hear about another anxiety attack?

My fingernails drummed out a melodic cadence as I typed my reply.

Erm... Not great really. I had another panic attack today after I'd finished picking up a couple of bits in the supermarket. They seem to be getting more regular. I don't really know what to do. Do you think I should speak to my doctor? xxx

I watched Jess's avatar drop down to my message as she read it, and then watched the dots bob rhythmically at the bottom of the message window as she wrote her response.

Yeah, definitely. It can't hurt. I've got a Wellbeing Workshop that I'm attending via Zoom at the weekend. Maybe you can join in with that? It might just give you some options to think about if nothing else. xx

I sat and mused about what a 'Wellbeing Workshop' even was, and how would that work over a Zoom call? Would I have to divulge my deepest and darkest fears? Talk about the anxiety attacks I'd been experiencing? Would we sit swaying and waving our hands about? I wasn't sure I was ready to bare my soul in front of a group of strangers, regardless of how small the group might be.

I don't know. What would I have to do? xxx

You just join the Zoom call and then the person running the workshop guides you through different activities and meditations. Stuff like that. xx

Meditations? Do you have to like, hum, and stuff? xxx

Jess replied to the message thread with a few variants of a laughing emoji.

No. Not unless you want to. They generally just guide you through how to breathe and scenes to view in your mind's eye like the sea lapping at a shore, or a beautiful meadow filled with wildflowers. I've always found them

96

soothing and relaxing. It can really help to visualise being
calm and serene when you're feeling angsty. Just to ground
and centre yourself.

Want me to forward you the invite? xx

I stared at the screen for a little while, wondering if I did want to give something like that a try. It would be weird being on a Zoom call with people I didn't know and meditating with them. Sharing personal airtime with people that could judge me. Opening myself up to analysing my internal anxiety and fears in front of strangers. What if I got emotional and it made me feel self-conscious?

But maybe Jess was right, maybe this was the sort of therapy I needed to challenge my inner demons, and I could learn some techniques to help lessen my anxiety? Discover how to confront those fears face on and begin to oppose my negative internal dialogue? At this point I didn't feel like I really had any other options open to me. I needed to take that leap of faith.

Yeah. Okay. I'll give it a shot xxx

§

I sat expectant for the workshop to start, the circle spinning whilst I waited for the host to let me in. I sat with the laptop on my knee, switching between wringing my hands, or fiddling with my hair, twisting it around my fingers absently.

Suddenly, the screen changed, and the workshop host

came into view, along with a couple of the other attendees.

"Hi, how are you?" a woman said as she examined the faces of the five others on the call.

"Erm... good thanks", I responded, readjusting my screen so I sat more central in the display, increasingly conscious of how I looked.

There was a chorus of similar greetings from the others on the meeting too, as they exchanged pleasantries. I searched for Jess, but she hadn't logged onto the call yet. My heart fluttered as I worried she'd forgotten all about it and wouldn't attend. But I needn't have worried as she came into view as an additional screen in the cluster of already open displays.

I gave a little wave, and she smiled and waved back.

"Right, ladies", our workshop facilitator said, "Let's get started. I'm Abbi and I would like to welcome you to this Wellbeing Workshop. Today we are going to do a little guided meditation, and hopefully I can get some feedback from you about your experiences here. I have done this a few times in the past now, mainly with young college-aged students, but because it's been so successful, I wanted to bring this to a wider adult audience. Is everyone okay with that and happy for me to proceed?"

We all either nodded or did a thumbs up.

"Excellent," Abbi smiled, "So let's begin the guided meditation. Have you all meditated before?"

Another chorus of agreements, whilst I sat there

shaking my head.

"Hi. Kerri... is it?"

I nodded, my cheeks flushing. I hoped the colour of my embarrassment wouldn't show through the camera. I needn't have been anxious, as Abbi gave me a reassuring smile.

"Don't worry, Kerri. This is a safe environment, and no one is judging anyone else. I will talk and guide you through the meditation, and we'll all have our eyes closed. No one will be watching you, so don't fret. Are you happy to carry on?"

"Yes. Thank you."

I sat back in the settee, shuffling my hips to make myself more comfortable and dispel any doubt I was feeling.

"Okay," Abbi started, "We'll begin. Sit back in your chair, making sure you're comfortable. Feel free to use pillows if you need to. Please make sure your feet are planted on the floor. Place your hands in your lap with your palms facing upwards. Close your eyes."

I closed my eyes, made sure I was comfortable and that my feet were flat on the floor.

"Just focus on the sound of my voice," Abbi continued softly, "as you begin to feel yourself relax. Take a long deep breath in, hold that breath and then slowly release it. Feel any tension you're holding ebbing away. Take another long deep breath. Hold. Exhale slowly and evenly. Begin to relax all your muscles, starting from your toes and feet, and working your way up slowly through your legs. Rest your back, release tension from your chest. Let your arms lie heavy in your lap and keep your palms upwards. Allow your shoulders to drop.

"As you begin to take another deep breath, I would like you to visualise yourself in respect to the Earth. As you visualise the Earth, you begin to see a stream of light coming up from the centre towards your feet. The light is yellow, bright and warm. Focus on that light leaving the ground and entering your body through the soles of your feet. As it enters through your feet, you feel the warmth of that light, and the soothing effect it has on your muscles."

I became aware of a far-off sounding voice sneering that this was a load of rubbish but shook my head gently to quickly silence it and fixated again on Abbi's voice.

"Envision that light moving from your feet, up your legs and filling your calves, heading towards your knees. As the energy reaches your knees, it turns from yellow to green. The green light travels from your knees, further up your legs, reaching your hips and spreading into the lower part of your stomach. As the green light spreads through your upper legs and thighs into your hips, it continues to warm your body and relax your muscles."

I was focusing so intently on Abbi's soothing tones that it wasn't difficult at all to imagine this light moving from the Earth through the lower regions of my body.

The sneering voice returned, probing at how this was

never going to work. I took another deep steadying breath, reminding myself that this voice was not helpful and blocked it with a smile as I enjoyed the control.

"The beautiful soothing light moves from green into a beautiful lilac colour as it reaches your navel and moves further up your torso and travels through your chest and heart space. The lilac light courses down your arms and glows fiercely as it comes out of your upturned palms. It moves up to your neck where it changes colour once more to the richest gold you've ever seen. This golden light bathes your face and comes out of the top of your head and flows all around the outside of your body to wholly encompass you, its caress warm to the touch, its beautiful hue soothing to your soul."

The sneering voice appeared for a third time, urgent in its quest to unseat me and push me towards anxiety and fear. I pushed the golden light surging through me towards it, searing the negativity with the positive energy I was feeling. This new source of power eviscerated the pessimism.

"Now that the golden light has surrounded you, push that light out to fill the room that you currently sit in. Push it into every corner of the room so that golden energy is filling every nook and cranny. Feel its warmth fill the space. Now push the light out even further, so that it fills and covers your whole house, making this space your safe space. A place for only you, your thoughts and your special cleansing, golden light. Sit in that energy now for a couple of minutes and enjoy the peace it brings you."

I sat there in my light and felt weightless, enjoying the warmth that had been a welcome surprise. I smiled to myself as I basked in the beautiful golden hue my mind had created. I became aware of my breath, moving slowly in through my nose and quietly out through my mouth. The sense of deep serenity and quietness of my mind. The lack of the sneering voice. Utter joy at the silence and peace within.

"Now bring that light back towards you. Allow the golden hue to change to a new colour, a colour your body feels it needs to show you. What colour is it? Is it a deep purple or a bright blue? Could it be a vibrant orange or a mossy green? Or have you brought through a range of colours like a rainbow? Let whatever colour emerges surround you; enjoy the colour you've created. This is the colour of your aura."

The colour I could see in my mind's eye was an incredible icy blue. So pure and bright that it was verging on brilliant white. It had threads of pink within it, like veins of gold running through a rock. It felt like a cleansing light and it was incredibly comforting to me. Something I had created and knew I would be able to find again. A new voice emerged, congratulating me on my positivity, telling me how strong I was. How proud it was that I was facing my negativity head on.

"Now allow that light to withdraw from everywhere you have sent it. Allow the light to flow from your head and arms into your chest and torso, moving further down into your legs and back into the floor. Watch it travel into the ground like roots into the centre of the Earth. Now that the light has gone, slowly come back to the room and when you're ready, open your eyes."

As I started to shift slowly where I sat, I wiggled my fingers to bring life back to them, moved my head from side to side to stretch my neck and then opened my eyes. The other people on the Zoom call were doing similar things to bring themselves gently back to consciousness, everyone with wide smiles on their faces.

Abbi looked from one screen to the other. "So how did you all find that?"

There were lots of nods and thumbs up as the other attendees expressed their appreciation for the guided meditation and said how calm they now felt, and that they were at ease and less anxious. How lovely it had been to see their auras and the different colours they had created.

Abbi thanked everyone for their time.

"I'll be running more workshops like this if any of you would be interested?"

We all nodded in agreement that we absolutely would.

"So, I'd just like a little feedback, whilst we're still on the call. Kerri, what will you take away from this workshop?"

I stared down at my hands in my lap as I considered my answer, the new internal voice melodic as it supported me to speak my truth. Encouraging me. Inspiring me. I looked up and beamed.

"I think the main thing I'll take away from this, Abbi, is that I have the strength inside of me to tackle my own fears head on. I don't need to give time or attention to negative thoughts. I have the ability to silence my own unhelpful judgements and pessimism. I can find the light and positivity I've been looking for inside myself, where it was all along, in the most unexpected of places."

The Price of an Open Heart

Maria Jerinic

Henderson, Nevada, USA

Early morning, I've been up since five, for my regular reading hour. Today, I finish a book about the friendship between Dorothy Sayers and C.S. (Jack) Lewis. I shelve it and prepare for my morning bike ride.

This has been my routine for most of the pandemic. I wake up early, the first one in the house, and I read. Then I ride. When I'm finished, I shower, dress, wake up my children, and get ready to teach online.

I don't always think about my reading once I put my book down. Instead, I think about the day ahead, plan, make mental lists of the many tasks I have once I return from the ride, even though we are stuck at home.

Today is different. On this day, while I prepare for my ride, the book runs through my mind, distracting me as I search for my gloves, bottle, and helmet. Is such distraction a problem? The text lives. Isn't that what I teach my students? "Use literary present tense when you analyze," I tell them. The author may long be dead, but the words, the ideas are timeless. We analyze a Shakespearean sonnet, and we use the present tense: "The poet writes…"

I fill my water bottle as I think about Sayers and Lewis, how they were not childhood friends, not close friends who were part of each other's daily lives. They conducted much of their relationship through letters. Yet Sayers' death filled Lewis with such grief. According to the writer, Gina Dalfonzo, "Jack Lewis's stepson Douglas Gresham recalls that the first time he ever saw Jack cry was when he heard about Dorothy's death."[2] Imagine the quality of their connection, the power of their words to each other, so strong that it could move Lewis deeply, that he felt such loss. Did his friends, his colleagues, his world understand such grief? Would our world? If I were to grieve the loss of my email friend, my writing partner, someone I connect with primarily through words, would people understand? Do we only understand the loss of a parent, a child, a lover? Do we understand the loss of a pet more than a friend?

My thoughts are interrupted by delays. All I want to do is ride my bike, but I discover one of my offspring has absconded with my earbuds, so I grumble and look for a new pair. Then I lift the bike off the stand to discover the chain has come loose, and I spend more time fiddling with that. All these obstacles when I just want to ride.

Finally, I climb on the bike and think about Lewis's tears. My children cannot say they have never seen me cry. My students too. I'll read them a passage and say, "isn't that beautiful?" as my eyes well up. I am easily moved to tears.

---

[2] Gina Dalfonzo. *Dorothy and Jack: The Transforming Friendship of Dorothy L. Sayers and C.S. Lewis.* Baker Books, 2020. p. 158.

What is different about today is that I want to cry in private, not in my house, not in the classroom, but out on the trail, on my bike where I am alone. I head toward a hill and crank up the resistance, so I have to strain to push the pedals. The heavier breathing, the dull ache in my thighs, the cold that settles on the back of my neck release the tension, and I cry while I pump my legs.

Later that day and I am back at my writing desk, trying to find words to describe my ride and my response to Sayers and Lewis and to my own impending loss. My friend is dying. Present tense. As I write this, she lies in bed across town, while slowly moving into the next world. By the time I finish a full draft of this essay, will her journey be finished? Will her life be past tense, or despite death will she still be in present tense? Will she continue to live, like the text?

My friend is dying in the midst of a pandemic but not from COVID-19. It is cancer.

How does one write about the loss of a friend? Tennyson's "In Memoriam," gives us one model: "'Tis better to have loved and lost / Than never to have loved at all." My students love this line and are shocked when I tell them it's not about romance but about Tennyson's love for his friend Arthur Hallam.

Still, I think my friend would prefer the version of Gilgamesh and Enkidu. She loves the ancients, having studied and taught them. I am sure we discussed Gilgamesh at some point. I know we talked about the Code of Hammurabi. I think she would appreciate the story of Sayers and Lewis. She appreciates the life of the mind, the thrill of thought and ideas. She is also reverent while not at all a traditional Roman Catholic. It has always been clear to me that despite her unconventional lifestyle, she has never abandoned her childhood faith.

How does one lose a friend during COVID? How does one comfort her? How does one help another into the next world when one cannot visit in this world?

So many obstacles hindered our visits: the rehabilitation home rules, her locked cell phone with my contact info her partner could not access, my germs from living in a house with so many people. All of these obstacles tied to COVID-19.

§

I started riding outside in response to the shutdown. Before that, I was a regular gym goer—7 days a week, usually some combination of spin and weight training. When I got the gym-closure email, I didn't panic while my kids, also avid gym goers, did. I tried to console them. "Just for a couple of weeks," I said. "We can make it through that." (Little did we know—as my kids like to point out - that we are still "making it through.") After all, we improvised our workouts when we traveled. So I considered our options. I pulled out all the weights from under our beds, found the weight benches in the garage, and I set them up in the family room. I ordered a complicated pullup structure that I put on the back porch along with an old aerobic step and a Pilates bar and stand. Then my father called and reminded me that he wanted me to take his bike, that at 80 he was not going to get on it again. He loved that bike. He had spent a lot on it and cared for it, and he wanted to share it with me.

I became an outdoor cyclist.

My first rides were long and usually flat, exploratory as I became used to riding outside. Now, at least several days a week, I ride to the pedestrian overpass where I meet my gym-friend. We chain our bikes to the railing, and I run the stairs while she runs the ramps. Then we switch, giving each other space, so we don't exhale all over each other.

I don't remember how or when I met K. We both taught for the same college. We taught the same course. Our paths intersected, and we shared readings and syllabi. Our friendship was centered on our campus life. At some point the professional academic world spilled over into the personal. We talked about ancient texts. We talked about our parents, our childhoods, about what to wear to what event.

We Americans love origin stories. Who are you, and how did you become the person you are? What problems did you face, and how did you triumph? We like these stories for relationships too, but just, I think, for romances.

How did you meet? When did this start? When did you know this was the ONE? How often do we ask these questions about friendships? Not often, I think. Is this because we only want to focus on that one relationship that lasts forever? Is it because, despite all evidence to the contrary, despite the statistics that tell us another story, we still believe in that one long-lasting exclusive relationship that will save us from loneliness, heartbreak, and loss?

I, on the other hand, love to hear those friendship-origin stories. I ask people to share theirs when they tell me about a good friend. I have some good ones of my own, but the one with K is not too exciting. I cannot remember when we first met. I have no memories of hurdles we faced or how we helped each other grow up.

K was not my oldest or closest friend. I feel that's important to say in a culture that only seems to value friendships when people are like "family." We say, "she was like my sister" or "sister from another mother," or "a brother to me." Why do we do this? A throwback to primal ties? I love my family, but those relationships are different. Why do we have such a hard time understanding a person's value in our life outside of ties of blood or sex?

K was not my oldest or closest friend, but she was my friend, and that is enough. We were not Enkidu and Gilgamesh or Tennyson and Hallam. Ours is not the story of a lifelong bond (I do have that story but with someone else), but it is a story of a friendship that matters to me.

Writing that statement helps me to remember that I have many such friends. Some are close; some are casual, but they buoy me in many ways, and I hope I do the same for them. Layers of friendship that warm me in different ways. I have the big loves, the old unwavering friendships, the newer social ones forged in the workplace or on a child's playdate; these connections matter. I need them all.

On some level, I have always known this to be true. COVID-19 has helped me to feel it. With our interactions so limited I have felt the holes, the absence.

§

I am back at my desk, and K has died. She is now past tense.

I was pulling on my tights, getting ready to visit her, when her partner texted me. I had one leg in one tight-leg. The other was bare. I heard the beep, looked at the text and sat down on the floor. I sat like that for some time, one leg in and one leg out of the trap of my tights.

She had slipped away two hours before, while I was biking. During that ride, I had thought about her, and unbidden, Rupert Brooke's words ran through my head: all his love for "cups" and "plates" and "raindrops." I realized I always think of K in terms of what she loves: ancient history, teaching (both history and aerobics), sports, rock music, concerts, PBS, traveling. She doesn't like spicy food or red wine or really any alcohol, so when we traveled for conferences, she would not join the rest of us on our culinary adventures. She chose room service.

She always asked me about my children's intellectual life: what were they interested in; what did they think about? These questions reflect something else she loves: the life of the mind.

She did not like Las Vegas. She did not want to retire here. I am sure she did not want to die here, but she did. There will be a mass? But when? A funeral? But when? The pandemic makes it difficult to plan. Where will she rest? Does it matter? Will there be, to use Brooke's words, "some corner of a foreign field" that will be "for ever"…what? "For ever" K?

§

I have always had an inflated sense of my own health. I rarely get sick, and when I do, I am shocked, astounded. I rail against some invisible germ force, "I don't have time for this." I am sure that one day I will be punished for this arrogance, but during this pandemic I have not worried about myself. What does worry me—that I could be a silent carrier, that I could expose someone else. That fear made me uncertain about how to care for K in her sickness. Over the summer we met and walked, had coffee outside. She so wanted to do this while I worried about her being out and about. She begged me, and we did all the things we were supposed to do: masks, distancing, hand sanitizer. Once she was confined to her apartment, I wanted to sit with her for hours, to hold her hand and to read to her. This was impossible because of COVID.

At the end, when I visited her in her apartment, I wore two masks and a face shield. I stayed across the room. I did not hug her. She sat in her wheelchair, boots on her feet and a hat on her head, dressed for errands she would no longer run, as if her clothes could keep her tied to this world. Was this her partner's attempt to keep her with him?

I reached over and squeezed her foot through her boot. "Remember" I shouted at her, "remember Phoenix? That time we walked into the Occupy Wall Street protest? Remember how they wanted to explain themselves, and you said, "no, you don't have to do that. We're with you?"

How ridiculous to shout at her like that, but otherwise how could she hear me from my distance and through my masks?

And she did hear me. During that one visit she nodded, acknowledging the story. She said my name. For the next visit, the last one, she was in bed, eyes closed, no longer in her street clothes. I hope she knew I was there. I shouted across the room, "Remember how much you loved that Dropkick Murphys song? Remember when you sang about the bells of Saint Mary's?"

It was during that last visit, I told her I loved her. Was this extreme, a dramatic gesture for my work friend? But there are many kinds of love. There are many kinds of friendship.

I have many kinds of friends in my life. One friend I have known for over fifty years. She lives on the opposite side of the country, but we are forever tangled up in each other's lives. I have two friends whom I met in graduate school. We were each other's family and support during those intense years. Now, they are neighbors to each other while I am across the country. We have been friends for three decades, and quarantine delayed my plans to visit them. When we talk, it is as if we are back in school, and no time has passed. When we text, the messages fly back and forth. One day one complained; "I saw a patient and during that one visit 29 messages piled up from you two."

There is another person from graduate school who is still my friend. Our bond was forged over discussions about books and poems and dreams and relationships. We still share these loves.

There are my friends who live near me, our connections forged on my children's soccer fields and at PTO meetings, at Serbian community events, and at work. I have three office friends, and we go out at least four times a year to celebrate our birthdays. Sometimes I worry what will happen when one transfers to another department. It is very possible that the intensity of our interaction will diminish, and this idea troubles me. Still, I remind myself, just because a friendship doesn't last does not mean it wasn't meaningful. Why does something have to be forever?

114

§

While I regularly design new routes for my long rides, my ride to the overpass is my most regular one. This is not a beautiful stretch of path. To get there I cross two busy streets, and only sometimes do cars honor the crosswalk and stop. The path runs behind a shopping plaza with a Walmart and Sam's Club. It's often littered with plastic bags. (Do people just rip into their purchases and toss the plastic?) Once, during the height of the BLM protests, I rode over fresh racist graffiti. I turned around and rode back over it, wondering whom I should call and almost smacked into a newly arrived newscaster and his camera person.

The next day, the graffiti was gone. Instead, I smelled baked goods coming from the plaza. Donuts always lift my spirits although it has been months since I let myself eat one.

This is the ride I took while K was slipping away, while she died, while she exhaled her last breath.

I wonder if I was on my bike when she passed. Did it happen after I hopped off and raced up the stairs? What was the exact moment that her spirit left her body? Did I ever feel a slight change in the atmosphere that signaled her departure?

No, I did not.

This idea continues to sadden me. People leave the earth, and we are unaware of the tremendous shift that has occurred in the universe.

§

It's easy to be irritated, to find our fellow humans too irrational, too selfish, too this or that. I ride my bike and see the homeless man sleeping on the sidewalk. How do we live in a world where this happens: a man sleeps on pavement in the cold? I see the woman who can't be bothered to leash her dog who pounces on me. I stop and speak with another woman who wants to argue about why she has to wear her mask in the gym.

Sometimes I want to shout in frustration. But am I so innocent? What about my many irrational selfish moments?

And there are also the people who smile at me, seeing me day after day. There are the other walkers who have started to join my gym-friend and me on the stairs, running a lap or two before continuing their separate journeys. My gym-friend and I have deepened our friendship with this time on the stairs. We don't see each other outside of exercise sessions, but we tell each other how grateful we are for each other's company during this pandemic.

§

Two months after her death, I joined K's partner to help him clear out her office. I thought this would be a day-long project. I thought we would both be reduced to tears. Instead, we were focused, efficient. Keep that picture; shred those gym fliers; recycle that pile of student papers.

What surprised me was that buried in the stacks all

around her office, I found signs of her and me. I found drafts of the talks we gave. I found three bound copies of the journal with our co-authored article. I found a pile of programs for the conferences we attended together. These details reminded me, reassured me that we were connected. Perhaps I better understood my grief that had seemed out of proportion.

Her partner asked me to go through her bookshelves to find the books she loved most. There were many old teaching anthologies and textbooks—donate those. However, I found books on Pliny, on Cicero, on the women Medieval mystics. I found Stephen Greenblatt's *The Swerve*. "These she loved" I said, pleased and surprised that I knew this. I also found stacks of her Catholic high school's newsletters. "I'll take those too," he said.

I knew more about K than I thought I did.

§

Late summer—my husband and I watch our old dog mourning our daughter's and then our son's departure for college. He lies at my feet, his head on his paws. If I mention their names, his head whips up. Uncharacteristically, he hunts for my daughter's stuffed animals, which he then proceeds to gnaw apart. I fret that his heart is broken, and I hope the results are not fatal. "This is the problem with pets," my husband says. He means the impending death, loss. We love a creature we know we will probably outlive (unless we have a tortoise). He wonders if love under such conditions is worth it.

But isn't this the condition under which we forge all our friendships? We will lose some to death but others to job relocation, to arguments, to moves, to growing apart. We have no guarantee that the friend we make today will be there all the way down the road. (Frankly, we have even less of that that guarantee for a lover.) My student R shared this Murakami quote with me: "Like flowers scattered in a storm, man's life is one long farewell."

The "long farewell"—that phrase is perfect. We say goodbye every day. If we accept this idea, well then, the threat of loss should not be a problem. Or at least not a big one. We can accept that our hearts will break, but still, we can celebrate our strength and hope. We love in spite of it all; we throw down our gauntlet in the face of certain loss. Love is not love that relies on guarantees, or love acknowledges one guarantee—there will be loss.

§

K is buried with her family in a Midwestern landscape she loved. Now it is the start of a new school year. COVID-19's Delta variant lurks, but the campus slowly comes back to life. I watch students stroll in groups across the quad. I watch them trail into the buildings, chattering animatedly. They tell me they are relieved to be back in physical classrooms. They are ready to make friends. They worry maybe everyone has made their friends already. It strikes me that they are applying their romantic ideals to their friendships, that perhaps they don't know another way to think about close bonds. They have learned to privilege the isolated couple, the couple against the world, that couple that one day might become the tight nuclear family with limited space for outsiders or third wheels. But exclusivity is not ideal for friendship. Friendships can build communities. They can pull us out of our isolated bubbles. They pose a challenge to the nuclear family model. They also expose us to more sadness and grief. We have more people to lose, and we don't want that. We want to protect ourselves. Brian Doyle, in his moving essay "Joyas Voladoras" (which my students love) writes "You can brick up your heart as stout and tight and hard and cold and impregnable as you possibly can and down it comes in an instant." I sobbed when I heard of Doyle's death although I had only met him on the pages of his work. Should I stop reading to protect my heart? Should I stop connecting?

I don't share all this with my students. I don't need to overwhelm them with my critique of Western culture. Instead, I say, "you are allowed more than one friend. You don't have to be monogamous. There is room in your life for new friends."

I hope this is true. I hope that maybe this past year and a half will help them expand their lives and their hearts, so they are open. I hope they can let people go in and out of

119

their lives without feeling betrayed or permanently broken. I hope they will not fear loss but understand it is the price of an open heart.

All in All

Erik Pihel

Mountain View, California, USA

My personal health crisis started seven months before the COVID-19 pandemic. In August 2019, I was diagnosed with stage-three colorectal cancer. A surgeon removed my tumor but not before some cancer cells had broken through the tumor wall and entered my bloodstream. I started chemotherapy to hunt them down. When coronavirus particles started moving across the Pacific in planes and ships from China to the United States, I'd completed ten of twelve treatments.

Monday, 9 March 2020
I'd read news articles about COVID-19 and had seen videos of desperate patients and frantic doctors in Wuhan, China. I assumed it was like the SARS outbreak in 2002 and would infect people mainly in East Asia, then disappear. But it was now moving across the world on buses, trains, ships, and planes.

In his novel *The Plague*, Albert Camus presents a fictional epidemic in a fictional town on the coast of Algeria. While not Camus's finest literary work, the novel contains insightful portrayals of the quarantined mind. The inhabitants consider their quarantine absurd and temporary, but for Camus, the human condition itself was

121

absurd and temporary. The novel's epidemic—hardly a temporary pause on normal life—highlights the true human condition: we are mortal beings whose death is always just around the corner.

More COVID-19 cases were discovered in the US, including my county. Like the inhabitants of Camus's town, some downplayed the virus's seriousness, while others became increasingly anxious about growing case numbers. Newscasters emphasized washing one's hands regularly.

I'd already been living with a fatal disease for seven months. I'd already changed my habits and washed my hands constantly to protect against colds and flu because my infection-fighting white blood cells were greatly reduced from chemotherapy. I was already living with a plague. It felt like the rest of the world now joined me.

Wednesday, 11 March 2020

The world began to disappear. Schools and stores closed; events were cancelled. Most of my team at work had started working from home two days ago. When I left the office in the evening, I was the only one on our side of the building. I put my laptop in my backpack and walked toward the exit, assuming I'd work from home for a week or two, then return to the office. As I walked the long carpet toward the stairs, I didn't realize I'd never work in that office again.

I drove home. My gym had closed due to the pandemic, so I walked for exercise. When I lived in New York, I walked everywhere—to the grocery store, laundromat, subway, bookstore, bar, restaurant—but here in Silicon Valley's suburbs, I hadn't walked further than a five-block radius around my apartment. I now discovered new streets lined with pines, redwoods, plane trees, and palm trees. There were fewer cars, but they drove much faster in the absence of traffic, racing through a shut-down world, a bizarre rush to nowhere.

The sidewalks I walked were emptied of people: fear had erased their bodies from the landscape. While shoppers talked with each other more often in grocery stores at the pandemic's start, the sidewalks were a different story. The sun shined warmly an hour before sunset, lighting trees and the few pedestrians scared of each other. When I saw people in the distance walk toward me, they usually crossed the street so we wouldn't pass each other. No one wore masks outside: it wasn't yet understood how well they reduced the virus's spread. My fellow pedestrians and I kept our distance from each other with little idea of what was safe and what was not but certain that other people were carriers of death.

Monday, 16 March 2020

Before my eleventh chemotherapy treatment, I drove to the blood lab. My white blood cell count dropped after each infusion. If my blood tests showed that my immune system hadn't recovered enough, then the treatment would be postponed. For the first time, a masked man stood at the door. "In the last two weeks," he said, "have you had a sore throat, fever, or cough? Have you traveled? Do you know

123

anyone who's sick?"

I answered no to his questions, and he let me in. A nurse drew my blood, and a lab technician ran tests, while I drove to the Cancer Center whose door was guarded only by a sign reminiscent of the one outside hell—"Abandon all hope you who enter here"—in Dante's poem:

Sore Throat? Fever? Cough?

Do Not Enter

Go Back to Your Car and Call For Assistance

I entered, walked to the infusion room, and sat for my treatment. My test results showed that my counts of white and red blood cells were low but high enough to proceed.

For the first time, doctors and nurses wore masks to prevent infecting cancer patients whose immune systems were compromised by chemotherapy drugs. Patients, however, did not wear masks. The current understanding was that a mask prevented the wearer from infecting others but didn't offer protection for the wearer. The Center for Disease Control was also concerned that if people panicked and bought many masks, there wouldn't be enough for medical professionals.

My masked nurse pushed a needle into the mediport that had been surgically implanted into my chest. The needle pricked and stung for a minute, then I didn't feel it anymore. The infusion machine dripped pre-medications—sugar water and steroids—into my vein for fifteen minutes.

My nurse then called another nurse and together they

double checked my name, my birthdate, and the chemicals they were about to inject into me. Once they'd confirmed that the plastic bag on the tray was indeed my toxin, my nurse connected Oxaliplatin, the venom, and Leucovorin, the antidote, to the machine. Up above, from a bag labeled *POISON*, Oxaliplatin dripped slowly into my chest, then into my bloodstream. This killer didn't select its targets nor could it distinguish cancer cells from normal cells. It dove into my blood and attacked every cell it encountered. A million cells died each second in a human body and this murderer added to the already staggering death toll. My cells would eventually replicate enough copies to replenish what had been lost: normal cells that knew when to stop dividing and died in the graveyard of a healthy body.

A patient walked by and sat in the station next to me. A nurse discovered she had a 101° F temperature, felt chills, and was breathing a bit heavier than normal, possible symptoms of COVID-19. I was alarmed that a possible carrier of the fatal virus had walked past me while my white blood cells were depleted. She now sat ten feet away exhaling into the room. She wasn't coughing or sneezing and probably didn't want to postpone her treatment, but she shouldn't have entered the building with her symptoms, let alone the infusion room with immuno-compromised cancer patients.

Two nurses wrapped a blanket around her and started to walk her out. She was too weak to walk, so they helped her into a wheelchair and wheeled her to another area in the building. The nurses returned, pulled the curtain around the chair she'd sat in, and cleaned the station. They seemed calm, which was reassuring.

They brought in more bleach and sanitizer. One phoned a supervisor, asking where they should send the patient. They discussed the screening process. "They've scaled it down to true droplets," one said. We still thought the virus was passed only as large droplets from sneezing or coughing, which fell to the ground quickly. The virus would be passed on if droplets landed on a doorknob, for example, and someone touched the doorknob and then touched their eyes, nose, or mouth. A few more weeks of research would show that singing and even talking sent droplets into the air, though their trajectory was much shorter than coughing and sneezing. We didn't yet know that COVID-19 also traveled on air currents for hours as tiny particles that could be inhaled, a much more infectious route.

"They should take their vitals outside," another nurse said. Currently, they followed the process they'd followed for decades: they measured our temperature, blood pressure, and pulse in the infusion room, checking our readiness for chemotherapy. If we weren't ready, we were sent home to rest, but our poor health was limited to our own bodies. Now there was a new disease that played by different rules. If it was discovered in the infusion room that we had a fever from COVID-19, it was too late: we were already spreading the virus to other patients.

I waited for COVID-19 symptoms to appear over the next few weeks, but they never arrived. Fortunately, I only had cancer.

Monday, 6 April 2020

Friends and family congratulated me on finishing chemotherapy, but it hardly felt like I was done. While my appetite slowly improved, other side effects continued full force. The neuropathy[3] in my hands and feet was worse than it had been during treatment.

While most of the world focused on COVID-19, I had more pressing things to take care of. My thumbs felt stiff and numb. If I stretched my hands, they tingled with neuropathy. The skin on my fingers felt like a constant sunburn. I dropped things more frequently. Two bowls had already shattered on the kitchen floor. It wasn't that I got distracted and dropped something or grabbed something more slippery than expected. I held something and then it was on the floor with no sensation of dropping it. I could no longer feel surfaces. When I touched something, I'd feel only the prickling in my fingers. Every surface, no matter how flat or smooth, felt like the rough stubble of an unshaven face.

---

[3] Neuropathy is nerve damage that causes numbness, stiffness, tingling, and pain, usually in hands and feet. It's a very common side effect of the chemotherapy drug I was given.

My feet were cold and I couldn't warm them, even with two pairs of wool socks and pointing a space heater directly at them. Two toes on my left foot were stiff and numb. It was sometimes difficult to maintain balance when standing still. It felt like my body was leaning forward and I'd have to reposition myself.

I woke once or twice a night covered in sweat. I changed the shirt I'd slept in. I didn't have a fever and felt fine, but something was being processed and released when my body heated while asleep. Once an hour during the day I felt an odd twitch in both calf muscles at the same time. It wasn't painful, but every new bodily sensation made me think *Is this the beginning of something worse?* Sometimes I felt my right hip heating up. My body was never at rest. There was often some odd sensation that had never happened before chemotherapy.

It felt like my body was not my own anymore. Foreign agents had taken it over. Gradually, it started to feel like I was taking care of someone else's body. I was like the custodian of a building, managing the needles and cold in this body's hands and feet, and dozens of other side effects. But I was not the building, and the building didn't belong to me.

Monday, 13 April 2020

My body continued its odd behavior. The twitching in my calves now sometimes shot down to my feet and it happened more frequently. Sometimes at night, before falling asleep, I wondered if, after closing my eyes, I'd ever open them again. In the morning when I opened my eyes, I was surprised to find my lungs still breathing and my heart still beating. Another day. Then a familiar fear returned that each moment could be my last. This had always been true but living with this awareness was paralyzing.

I didn't trust my body. It seemed like it didn't know what it was doing or how to respond to the invasion of poisons. I was inside an unstable structure that could collapse at any time and need an Emergency Room. This triggered events from my past.

When I was eleven years old, I sat inside the house in Connecticut that I'd grown up in. A storm whipped the windows with wind and rain. While the storm was more intense than usual, it was still in the realm of normal for autumn. Then my ears locked and wouldn't unlock. The house became strangely quiet for ten seconds, then exploded. I opened my eyes and saw that I was flying in open, roaring, wet air, surrounded by broken walls and furniture that were flying too. *I must be dreaming*, I thought, but it felt real. I continued hurtling through the air and shouted a prayer to God in the thundering wind to "Please help me." I flew deeper into the unknown at a mind-erasing velocity, then everything stopped moving. The world stopped roaring as I laid on a broken closet with piles of my mother's clothes. The wind had stopped, but rain continued to pour down. I climbed down from the rubble and looked at my street. Houses on the left side had disappeared, while those on the right remained. The sky was low, dark clouds. The world had turned dark and unrecognizable. A quiet, suburban street in Connecticut had turned into a war zone. As the neighborhood refugees found shelter in a house still standing, I was astonished that the adults knew what had happened and named the events a *tornado*. They had a name for the unnameable mystery of sitting in an exploding house, flying through the air, and landing in a new world.

Later, as an adult on September 11th, 2001, I stood on Hudson Street in Manhattan's Soho district and watched the World Trade Center towers burn. Unlike most of the world, I didn't watch it on TV listening to broadcasters making up stories. Without incessant narratives, the flames radiating from buildings, exhaling smoke, were meaningless. We call images of the burning towers *powerful symbols*, but the images' significance was created entirely by language: the stories inside the minds of hijackers, passengers, and office workers; the stories of strategists in Afghanistan and Pakistan; the stories of responders in Washington DC. When I watched the pre-story, burning towers, the sound was turned off with no play-by-play commentary. Just the wail of an occasional siren, and the eerie, indecipherable visuals that made no sense whatsoever. The only significance of those images was the temporary nature of the entire material world. I watched the towers burn as they'd burned in cities throughout history in Troy, Babylon, Rome, Alexandria, Jerusalem, and Constantinople.

"The world is on fire," Buddha says in "Old Age," while we casually laugh, wrapped in an illusion of permanence. Our minds burn with desires and fears, mistaking the temporary for the permanent. "All things," he says in "The Fire Sermon," "are on fire [...] with the fire of passion." We live inside our desires and fears, distracted from our slow march toward death, but our very lives are on fire "with birth, old age, death." The material world decomposes into ashes, but we continue to view it as the solid rock of reality. A house felt safe on a rainy autumn afternoon, then exploded in the wind. Steel buildings seemed solid on a clear autumn morning, then New York's tallest buildings rushed down and disappeared into the Earth.

Now I had these same feelings of instability about my body, blown by random winds and burning in unpredictable ways. Even minor sensations had the potential to grow into life-threatening storms. The house I lived in—my body— was hit by odd sensations that foreshadowed emergencies. While one could run down steps to a basement before an oncoming tornado or exit a burning building, there was no escape from my own body. There was no exit from myself.

I sat inside this unstable house, unfamiliar sensations threatening to bring the entire house down. I looked out at the horizon, and death stared back. I looked out over the edge of my life and wasn't ready to fall out of the world.

Monday, 20 April 2020

I was scheduled to start radiation treatments to burn cancer cells that might have escaped surgery and chemotherapy. I drove to the Cancer Center for a mapping: a precise outline—to the millimeter—of my body's area that would be irradiated to ensure the linear accelerator fired X-rays into exactly the same places each time. I parked and walked toward the building, stumbling a few times. Neuropathy in my feet and nervousness about radiation made it difficult to balance.

A nurse outside the building asked if I had an appointment, where I was going, and the usual COVID-19 questions, except now the symptoms also included chills, stomach pain, and diarrhea. And now she checked my temperature with an infrared thermometer gun pointed at my forehead. My temperature was normal, and I walked to the Cancer Center. A masked nurse called my name and led me past medical oncology's infusion room to the radiation oncology wing.

I had a deep respect for nurses from my surgery and chemotherapy, but COVID-19 nurses during the pandemic shined in their brightest radiance. They were the front line in a war against an invisible enemy, dressed in battle gear: two masks, hood, face shield, scrub gown, plastic apron, and two pairs of gloves. Their red-lined faces from masks at the end of a shift were battle scars of this war. They were our soldiers, terrified of getting infected and infecting others, holding a phone so that relatives could say goodbye to a dying patient, feeling helpless as a patient died in their care, and staying away from their own families to avoid spreading infection.

In some parts of the world, people whose fear of contagion had severely distorted their thoughts threw rocks at nurses, threw chlorine and bleach into their faces, and threatened them with rape. They walked past this confusion into hospital rooms where patients thanked them and whispered "I love you" between gasps for air. They saw fear in patients' eyes just above the intubator. Their compassion awakened, they rushed past their own fears to comfort the dying. Patients looked up into the eyes of the last human being in a changed landscape, their ambassador to the next world, a masked stranger who held their hand as they exited their life.

I sat on another front in the slower, longer-term war of cancer. Doctors and nurses at the Cancer Center had been wearing masks to prevent infecting cancer patients with COVID-19 since mid-March. It was now understood that masks also offered protection for the wearer and so patients were now required to wear them. I'd never worn a mask before but had purchased a cloth mask in 2017 to protect against smoke from fires in northern California. This mask that I hadn't used—two straps for wrapping around the back of my head and neck—was too tight and fogged my glasses.

I inhaled through the suffocating mask, my fingers and toes cold and tingling in the frigid air of the sanitized room, afraid of catching COVID-19 in a medical facility, and anxious about the radiation therapy to come.

"Do masks come in different sizes?" I said. "This one's too tight."

"No," my nurse said. "There's one size. I don't have any extra, unfortunately."

"Oh no, I don't want to take any from you."

She stood silently for a few moments, then said, "You look uncomfortable." She stepped outside and returned holding a paper bag with a single mask inside. "It's clean and sanitized," she said.

"Sorry for being unprepared."

"Here." She held the bag closer. "I always have a few extra hidden away."

I took off my mask and pulled the thin surgical mask out of the paper bag, which had loops for wrapping around my ears. I hurried to put it on so she wouldn't have to wait, though she showed no signs of impatience. My neuropathic fingers kept fumbling with the mask. "Sorry," I said. "My fingers are messed up from chemotherapy." It was embarrassing to be unable to do such a simple thing.

"Take your time," she said.

I wasn't looking at her as I tried to move my fingers around the mask loops but could sense that my suffering from chemotherapy and mask struggles had activated her compassion. I felt empathy radiating toward me. I didn't have to hear her speak or even see her eyes above her mask. It was a wave that I could feel, an underlying current with a slight vibration that connected us beyond the temporary roles of nurse and patient. The room felt infinite for a moment.

"It looks like you have it upside-down," she said. "There's one side for your nose."

I took it off, rotated it, and put it on again.

"And pull the other side down over your chin."

I pulled the mask down.

"There you go."

"This one fits much better," I said. "I'll order some. Thank you."

Thursday, 30 July 2020

Three months later, I'd finished and recovered from radiation treatments, though side effects from chemotherapy continued. I was now an expert at mask wearing. I looped my surgical mask around my ears, pressed it around my nose to prevent my glasses from fogging, and stepped outside for my daily walk. I walked to the end of my block, then turned left onto a long, empty straightaway between the police station and train tracks that had no side streets, houses, or parked cars. It would have no sudden appearance of pedestrians, so I took off my mask and inhaled the fresh, clear, unfiltered air. It was odorless yet had a clean sweetness I'd never noticed before. A breeze

135

dried the perspiration around my mouth. The scent of the Earth filled my nose and mouth with energy. It was only when masking turned it off and unmasking turned it on again that I sensed how extraordinary the pure, ordinary air was. If only it were this simple to remove the mask of my thoughts and walk with a clear, unfiltered mind.

A couple appeared in the distance walking toward me. I put on my mask to protect them from my breath. I inhaled through the fabric and stepped off the sidewalk to provide more space. They were unmasked and passed as if I wasn't there. A thought arose: *You aren't doing your part.* My mind's masks continued to arise between me and fresh, clear, unfiltered awareness. I continued walking. Not there yet.

Sunday, 9 August 2020

I'd completed my treatments and there were currently no signs of cancer, but the fear of recurrence was stronger than ever. I'd been feeling pain in my knees, back, and neck, and had concluded that cancer had spread into my bones. My lack of training in bone cancer didn't stop me from believing this medical diagnosis, and once I'd definitively explained my symptoms to myself, my fear and anxiety intensified.

I woke in the morning. I was calm, then remembered I was in a body that felt pain. Fear and anxiety restarted. I stood and the feelings spread with a tingling as if the neuropathy in my hands and feet had moved through my entire body. I felt a pain in my neck. Before cancer, I'd tell myself, *It's nothing; it'll pass.* I assumed my body would recover from any ailment; I wouldn't visit a doctor unless the ailment persisted for several months. But a year ago, my stomach aches hadn't gone away and turned out to be cancer. Now my fears had more evidence to keep churning.

I saw my guitar leaning against a wall and remembered music, a potential way out of my psychological torment. I picked up my guitar and played a song I'd written many years ago about running on Brooklyn's sidewalks. The guitar strings dug into my neuropathic fingers, but I played through the pain. My song absorbed my attention.

I felt a headache but ignored it. My mind was conditioned to react immediately to pain signals, and it took will power to resist this instinctual reaction. I knew I had intermittent headaches—this wasn't new information—and didn't have to respond to each signal with a story of brain or bone cancer. Instead, I stayed inside my music where everything was fine.

Usually I didn't like hearing myself sing, but for the first time in my life, I liked how my voice sounded. My voice was the right voice for this song. The lyrics had come from a deep part of me, and now I reconnected with that part as I sang. I continuously created the music that enveloped me like a wavering blanket of light. I'd returned to my own creative power. I'd replaced the story of a helpless patient dying of cancer with the music of an older self, a pre-cancer self, chords and vocals from an earlier time when I lived in

New York and wrote songs rather than managed side effects from cancer treatments. I strummed the chords of a pre-COVID age, brought them into the present, and lived in that music for a moment.

Wednesday, 2 September 2020

My eyeglasses had enough scratches that soon I wouldn't be able to see through them. I'd scheduled an eye exam and drove to the eye doctor's office. Everyone in the office wore masks to protect against COVID-19, but still I was anxious about breathing in numerous small rooms with multiple people. The rooms were air conditioned, which was comforting, but still I imagined corona particles lingering as I looked through machines at tiny letters and flashing lights. My doctor confirmed that my eyes didn't have cataracts, glaucoma, or retinal tears.

I stepped into the main room and quickly picked out new frames to leave as soon as possible.

The five other people all seemed calm as if death wasn't haunting the room. A man chatted with an assistant as he waited for his wife to return from her exam. For them, the thin curtain between life and death hadn't been shredded by cancer. They talked as if they were immortals casually passing eternity on Mount Olympus.

I wanted to escape this death chamber. "Can we do the rest over the phone?" I asked the assistant processing my order.

"No," she said. "I have to measure your eyes. It won't

take long."

It took an eternity. My desire to get out of the office slowed time to a geological scale. She clamped a measuring device onto the new frames. I put them on, and she took my picture with a tablet. Then another picture. She stared at the tablet quizzically. Eons passed. Glaciers solidified, then melted back into the ocean. "I have to do it again," she said. Two more pictures, then more staring at the tablet. She had the patience of a centipede inching across sands of the Sahara. "You can take them off," she said. "We're finished." But we were far from done. I placed the frames on the table as she stared at a paper and tapped the tablet one letter at a time like a medieval monk tracing each stroke of a sacred text.

I imagined corona particles moving through the air. "I'm going to wait outside," I said and walked through the door into a breeze where many cars passed emitting carbon monoxide but only a few pedestrians potentially exhaling COVID-19.

Ten minutes later, she called me in again. She pressed the screen on the cash register to charge my credit card.

I put my card on the counter to speed things up.

She ignored my card, even though it was the main point in this phase of the geological cycle. She tapped the screen. New species evolved while others died off. She finally picked up my card. Instead of using an automatic card reader— invented four decades ago—she looked at each number, then tapped the corresponding number on her screen. Then she slowly tapped numbers from a paper into her screen as if she wanted to savor every moment we had together. A long paper receipt slid out of a machine. "That's for the eye exam," she said. "Now I'll do the frames and lenses."

It felt like she was torturing me. *It's okay*, I told myself. I inhaled deeply and slowly exhaled. I stopped trying to rush her with my mind. Time stopped for a moment, and I no longer felt anxious. It seemed like the room's walls were flowing away from me. Then my anxiety returned.

She tapped the screen for each digit. Another long paper receipt slid out of the machine, and she released my card onto the table.

I took the receipts and my card, said "Thank you" in the brightest tone I could manage, then walked quickly out the door.

Wednesday, 9 September 2020
The marine layer along the US's Pacific coast is a stable air layer that forms over the ocean after sunset. It moves inland at a steady altitude of 2,000 feet, creating a channel of clean air from the ocean into coastal areas, producing some of the cleanest air on Earth. The heat of the morning sun burns away this marine layer, leaving blue sky.

In the darkness of night, fires burned along foothills of the Sierra Nevada mountains. Sudden, strong winds blew smoke straight up into the atmosphere to 40,000 feet, higher than the altitude of commercial airplanes, where the air is frigid. The fires created their own weather system, forming clouds of smoke, ash, and ice high in the atmosphere. Strong winds carried this fire storm southwest to San Francisco's Bay Area.

Smoke and ash descended to the marine layer and mixed with its thick moisture. As our slice of the Earth turned toward the morning sun, this toxic cloud prevented much of the sun's heat from reaching the surface, and so the marine layer didn't dissipate as it usually does. Instead, it provided a blanket between smoke and residents and continued to channel clean air from the ocean. Thick smoke particles scattered blue light and allowed only red, orange, and yellow light to filter through. What would have been a clear blue sky became an overcast, dystopian world.

I saw dim light behind my window shade shortly after sunrise. I opened the shade but didn't see the first streaks of sunlight above the horizon. Instead, I saw an eerie, orange world that was neither day nor night but a Martian landscape outside of time.

Atypically for my suburban neighborhood, one neighbor had a rooster who always crowed fifteen to twenty minutes after sunrise. This morning, the rooster didn't crow as if his innate sense of the sun detected no light source. Earth's solar compass was gone, and we were left spinning aimlessly in an orange glow. Hinduism names our current age the Kali Yuga, "Time's time," a dark age when caretaker gods retreat to let Time (Kal) operate on its own. The solar god retreated, and a region named *The Sunshine State* was left to spin on its own down whatever paths might be found.

The air looked odd, but the air quality was good because the marine layer protected us from the atmosphere's smoke. I put on a mask for the other apocalypse (the pandemic) and walked through the eerie glow to a market. Two women sat outside a café, eating breakfast in the orange air. They chatted as if it was a normal day, but their breakfast items in this strange context reminded me of hotel silverware covered in ash on 9/11. I bought fruit and yogurt, then walked homeward.

I looked at the orange sky and imagined that centuries ago, without meteorologists' explanations, I'd have looked at this sky and wondered what had happened to the sun. I might very well have thought the end was near. We still posted such sayings online, but they were jokes because we were protected by scientific explanations. *Apocalypse* was an ancient Greek word that means an un- (*ápo*) hiding (*kálupsis*), a revealing of what had been obscured. We'd outgrown revelations so that apocalypses were jokes or science fiction.

I arrived home and sat. I ignored explanations and gazed the strange sky through my window. Our blue world had been replaced by an orange one. I resisted my mind's tendency to explain and just let the stimuli paint my retinas. An orange canopy hung over an unfamiliar world. Soon I forgot what year it was and what planet I was on. I stood into this alien world like an explorer at the edge of space and looked out the window. I saw no people in this deserted landscape. Just abandoned streets and parked cars. A planet once inhabited was now filled with empty shells of a lost world.

I slowly emerged from my reverie. In the afternoon, I put on my mask and went for a walk. Through my mask, the air seemed fine. The streets were deserted, so I didn't need to protect anyone from my breathing. I took off my mask, but the air had an odd smell. I detected a tinge of smoke but inhaled mostly a chemical, industrial smell as if someone had just painted the world and the paint hadn't dried yet. Even though the air was clear of thin smoke particles that damage human lungs, it didn't feel right. I put on my mask, turned around, and walked home.

The marine layer dissipated. Ash and smoky, hazardous air descended to Earth's surface. I closed all my windows and pushed towels into the openings between the front door and wall to prevent outside air from coming in. I didn't step outside again until the air improved four days later. I had enough food for a few weeks. I mostly sat in my bedroom, the smallest room, with the door closed. My air purifier ran all day and night in this monastic cave while I wrote, dialed into work meetings, and composed songs.

Sunday, 13 September 2020

The air quality finally improved, so I stepped outside. I hadn't fully appreciated walking on the sidewalk until it was too dangerous to leave my apartment. Now the air smelled of pine, no longer disguised by dystopian odors from strange gods. I walked past redwood trees that didn't seem affected by their burning cousins to the southwest, one of three large fire complexes. They continued to stand rooted in the Earth.

My body felt strong. I walked a little faster. It felt like I was emerging from what cancer patients call *cancer brain*. Usually, the term refers to how chemotherapy drugs create distraction and forgetfulness in patients. I didn't experience any of that. For me, *cancer brain* was a psychological state where I thought of myself as a helpless victim of a fatal disease. It now felt like I had a little more time in this beautiful world. Yes, cancer cells might have escaped surgery, chemotherapy, and radiation, and were now moving through my bloodstream. Yes, the air was poisoned by a dangerous virus. Yes, there were three large fires and hundreds of smaller ones burning all around. But my lungs were still breathing oxygen, my heart still pumping blood, and my brain's neurons still firing electrical signals across synapses. I'd become aware of what the Earth's air smelled like for the first time. I'd rediscovered my own music. I'd felt compassion emanating from others as well as from deep within myself. All in all, it had been an interesting year.

Interview with Erik Pihel and Maria Jerinic

Finding Light in Unexpected Places, Volume 1

Carey Peña

24 August 2020

https://careypenareports.libsyn.com/finding-light-in-unexpected-places

Transcribed by Antonela Verdha

Carey Peña: Hi everyone. I'm Carey Peña, and thank you so much for checking in with us for this edition of our podcast *Carey Peña Reports*. And I am joined now by Maria Jerinic and Erik Pihel, the editors of a book called *Finding Light in Unexpected Places: An Anthology of Surprises*. Maria, thank you so much for being here. I know you're in Las Vegas. and Erik you're in California. Thanks to the both of you.

Maria Jerinic: Thank you. Thank you so much.

Erik Pihel: Thank you.

CP: Maria, I want to start with you. Well, first, you're a professor there at UNLV, and I understand that today was your first day back in school. How'd that go?

MJ: Yeah. Well, I'm sitting in my office right now. It was quiet on campus. I went into a class, and we're there with our masks and social distancing, and I asked the students, "How are you?" and they said, "We're excited to be in a classroom again." So, it was good. Baby steps. We'll see how the semester goes.

CP: Tell us how this book came to be.

MJ: Well, I was in a training session right before the semester started a couple of years ago, and the person running the training (we acknowledge him in our Acknowledgements) asked a question about those positive moments that you would relive, whether they are seconds or minutes. And I realized—I know I've had many in my life—but I was having a hard time recalling them. And I thought, *This is terrible! I'm always looking for the possible problems that can arise, trying to circumvent them, that I'm not spending enough time thinking about those really beautiful moments.* And I remember, after that meeting, going to Costco, doing my shopping, and I started texting Erik, *What if we...* somehow it involved that *...what if we somehow put this into writing?* Or I was sharing with him that I can't believe I had this reaction because Erik and I have been friends for a very long time. And so somehow in that texting conversation, standing by the paper towels, the idea to do this call sort of came about. And that's how I remember it. Erik, how about you? Do you have additions because sometimes we remember different things about these events?

EP: Well, I think we were thinking about the same topic in parallel without really knowing we were doing that. I had a slightly different angle on the same thing, and I've always been interested in finding interesting things happening in places you don't expect. So, we all know that if you look at a sunset, we look at a rainbow on top of a mountain—it's beautiful. That would be finding light in an *expected* place. But I've always been fascinated when you can find that same kind of light and joy and radiance in places that you don't expect, and, if the book is any indication, it seems like the two main contexts for that are either the tragic or the mundane. So you either have a tragedy and you find something beautiful within the horror, or you're in some very mundane and boring environment and something interesting happens out of the blue, unexpected. And so, I've been always interested in that. So when Maria told me that, well, I was thinking about the same thing: we should get a book together.

CP: And in the book, fourteen authors share their experiences of finding light in unexpected places. How did you go about finding the authors to share these stories, and then—Erik let me stick with you for a second and then I'll ask Maria about this a little bit more—but then from there, after you found the authors, how do you find those stories, the mundane or perhaps the tragedy that ends up being a bit of light?

EP: Yes. We put out a call, which just means you write up a description of the book, and you post in every possible place you can, and writers go to those websites and they look and think, "Oh, I have a story like that" or "I have already written a story like that," and they just came pouring out. So, some of those stories were about very famous events, like 9/11 or the Mexico City earthquake a few years ago, or the northern California fires a few years ago. People already had those stories in their minds, and then when they saw the call, they were triggered to write them. And so, that's how we went about the process, the editorial process, of gathering the stories together.

CP: Maria, what stands out to you when you started receiving these stories?

MJ: Well, as Erik said, on the one hand, it was partly some of those large events, to see a spin. There's one on Foley the journalist who was murdered, and I just remembered when that had happened. I'm originally from New England, and he almost felt like the boy next door. I found that very moving, because the writer really explored that, plus the theme of friendship which, for me, as I look at all these stories and I reread them, I realize how much our joy and our light comes from the communities that we have and the time we spend with other people. And so that, for me at this moment, poses an interesting problem when we cannot gather together as I think our human impulse is to do that, and more and more research is coming out talking about how much our bodies are wired to receive joy, in a sense. There's a biological reaction, oxytocin increases—I mean, I'm not a scientist but this is in the research that I've been reading—just by making eye contact and smiling at one another and spending time together. And these stories really reinforce that, that in these times it's when people, strangers or friends, somehow are able to reconnect, that we can find some of that light. And now we have to think of creative ways to do that in this situation that we're facing right now.

CP: Well, how interesting that the two of you came together with this concept long before the pandemic hit, and in researching some of the reviews and reading about your book, I read that "Wherever you are, whatever thoughts might be racing through your mind, light is available." Erik, right now for a lot of folks, they don't see much light. They don't feel much light. It's just a lot of darkness and a lot of fear.

EP: Yeah. I think it's easy to overlook. I have actually a very brief story about yesterday when I had one of these moments. So, I'm in northern California right now and there are fires burning everywhere. A week ago, we had like 11,000 lightning strikes that created like 400 fires, and some of these fires are now combined into large, complex fires, and one of these is burning about seventeen miles south of where I am. And so, last night was very hectic for the Bay Area because we were forecast for more lightning strikes. So more fires, more wind blowing things around, and in the middle of all that, around eight o'clock last night, a gentle rain started falling on the fire. And this woman tweeted a line from Shakespeare's *A Merchant of Venice,* where "The quality of mercy is not strained, it falleth as the gentle rain from heaven," and it was beautiful! It was such a moment of relief in all of that anxiety, all of that fear and, yes, it only lasted a few minutes. The rain moved on, and about ten minutes later, I got the rain here and then moved on again, so it didn't stop the fire, right? But it still, in that moment, gave a little bit of hope like, "We *can* get through this," like "We *are* going to make it through this." And some people, even on Twitter, were very cynical: "Oh, it just lasted for two minutes. Great, now we have to worry about the lightning strikes again." That's the normal human response. It's to say, "It didn't do anything. Let's just ignore that little two-minute window there and focus on the tragic and the fear and the anxiety." But if you pay attention, it's there, even in the darkest moments.

CP: Erik, do you think that too often we, as a society collectively, are looking for these *big* moments, these, like you said, the incredible double rainbow or the vacation to end all vacations, and, what I'm gathering, part of what you want to accomplish is saying to people, "What happened today, that might have been beautiful? Did you have a phone call with an old friend?" You know, just something maybe very, very simple?

EP: Yeah, I think it takes effort. That's the thing. It doesn't happen naturally. Maria was talking about biology. I think we're biologically wired to focus on the negative. You know, when we were on a savannah, the people who focused on the negatives—that saber tooth tiger over there, "I'd better get on the tree"—those are the ones that survived, and the ones that are just playing in the grass got eaten and didn't survive, and so we have this biological wiring to focus on the negative, because you say, "Ok, if I focus on that dangerous thing, I'm going to be safe," but the thing is, we're not in the savannah anymore. We have these appendixes that we needed when we were eating bark, right? We don't eat bark anymore, for the most part, and so there are things in our biology that might not be as relevant as they used to be. And so it's going to take effort to override that wiring and to always—you know, sometimes, yes.

151

Right now I have to be careful. I have to know where the fires are as does everyone else in my area, and so I need to be aware of that, but it's very easy to have that overwhelm you and just become obsessed with looking at the air quality, the movements of the fire all the time. I mean, that's just overwhelming. So it's good to know, like "How do I not do that twenty-four hours a day and only do that only like twenty-two hours a day?" And then have a little bit of time off to focus on something else, like watch a funny movie, or anything, or listening to some music. Because you can't: it's not possible to live that way all the time, and I think it takes effort.

CP: You know, and it makes me think of this wonderful family who I've done several interviews with. They live in the Phoenix area, and their daughter has a rare genetic disorder called Pitt-Hopkins Syndrome, and she's five and can't walk or talk, yet—they're obviously holding out hope there—but the mom, Nicole, said to me once, "Carey," because I also have little kids, and she said, "Carey, with Alexandra, we don't look for milestones. We look for inchstones, and every inchstone is something to be celebrated." And, in a way, I'm thinking of these writings that you all so beautifully put into this book to say, "Let's look for those inchstones." And even if it is getting out of your house, maybe going to your favorite grocery store after not venturing out too often. Maria, for you, in reading through these stories and editing this book, what have *you* learned?

MJ: Well, it shows me that the genre—here's the English teacher in me—this essay form is really something that goes back, arguably, to the sixteenth century with Montaigne. Some people will say that there are earlier examples of it. And the form is not the academic essay that we spend so much time on with students or a white paper, but the function of this genre really *is* to have, to focus, on those small moments, that surprise, revelation, or epiphany, that comes through when you're actually beginning to think about or talk about something else. So, for me, it's exciting to see how that genre is still living, and it's serving us very well in that way, and that as these writers were writing and revising, were talking about things, that that process of actually writing is what can help many of them find those moments in those reflective moments. And it reminds me of how important it is, since I tend to scan a lot as I said, and I appreciate seeing how other people write about it, how important it is to keep that practice up in my own life, even if it's completely private, so that I do focus on those moments, on those moments of joy and on the beauty, and not the primal fear that...I mean, I think Erik is right: we're wired on some level to survive that way. But also, it's interesting that our bodies do react very strongly to those positive moments of connection and light. So, we're still conflicted in those ways, and that's one of the beautiful parts of being human.

CP: A friend of mine, Lisa Menegatos, works with you, Maria, there on the campus of UNLV, and she's the one who brought this book to my attention. And I texted her, and I asked her, "What are your takeaways?" Being a professor, she sent me a very long text, so I'll just read you the last portion of it. She says: "The things that give us joy might look at lot different than they used to, or maybe we have come to better appreciate the mundane and ordinary in new ways, but the joyful moments and silver linings are there, *if* we look." And I thought that was really on point.

MJ: Yes, yeah. As Erik said, it takes effort. You have to look for it.

CP: Erik, what do you hope people learn from this book? And after we talk about that for a moment here, I do want to talk about the second book, because you have a call out for people to submit their stories. But, what do you hope people learn if they pick up—and this would be a great gift to give, I feel, if people are thinking about the holidays and spreading some joy, this would be a good gift—but, what do you want people to take away?

EP: Well, I think for a lot of people right now, it's a very dark time, especially with the pandemic, but there's a lot of other things going on as well, and I think it's very easy to lose hope. So, I would hope that they take away the fact that even when things seem hopeless, they might not be. And if you can read other people's stories about being in a dark place—it might not be your dark place—and they found their way out of it or at least found some break from it, like, you said, the inchstones versus the milestones. That's a great example. We might be looking for milestones, constantly thinking, "Oh, I can't run a marathon." I say, "Well, try running the sprint and see how that goes, you know? That's also an accomplishment." And so I think this will hopefully inspire people, even if they're not writers, to be able to at least take a second look at their circumstances and maybe things will go better. If I can just say one other brief story—I know that we haven't started talking about the second book yet, but it's about COVID-19—and I had one potential author, who was interested in the topic, who has had COVID-19 and recovered. And he was saying, "Well, I don't see any light in this at all, you know? I'm alive. I guess that's it." And I said, "You know, maybe not." And what I would say to that is that there's a book by Viktor Frankl called *Man's Search for Meaning*, and he was a prisoner in a Nazi concentration camp in World War II. And instead of talking about the dramatic moments of that concentration camp, he focused on the everyday life of that concentration camp, the little moments of the way that people interacted with each other—the way that the prisoners interacted with each other—and the thing that struck me the most about this book is that there's one scene where everybody in the camp is put into a train and they're all kind of heading in the direction of a very notoriously bad concentration camp, and they're all very fearful that they're going to that camp. Probably they're all going to die if they go there. And, at some point, the train turns away from that camp toward another camp and, Frankl describes, people started dancing on the train. They were so happy because they weren't going to the really bad camp. They were just going to, you know, a medium-level concentration camp, and the fact that that can even happen in one of the worst moments in all of human history, should tell us that, no matter what's going on with you, there must be something. If they can dance on a train like that, we can all find something in the darkest moments of own lives. And that's what I would hope people get from these books.

CP: You've had a good reception for the first book, so much so that you are working on a second. So, tell us a little bit more about that. Erik first and then I'll go over to you, Maria.

EP: Yeah, so this one is centered around COVID-19, and one of the things that I find interesting about this pandemic, is that it has touched every person on the planet. And you could argue that there is no other event that has quite done that before. The fact that every single person either knows someone, or COVID is in their neighborhood somewhere, or they've heard about it …that is incredible! That is an incredible moment in human history! And so it would be very curious to hear, *Oh, what is an experience like in Paris? What is an experience in Calcutta, India?* We're in all these different places and there's going to be commonalities, of course, but there's also going to be differences, and I'm actually interested to see what comes in from the submissions, to see what these experiences are because I don't know what it's like to be in India with COVID-19, but someone in India does. And to kind of give a global perspective of this would be my hope. I hope we get enough international submissions that we do get a global perspective on this pandemic and what it means to different people and different parts of the world.

CP: And Maria, will it also have the component that you're looking to continue to look for the light?

MJ: Oh, absolutely! After the book came out, many people wrote us, just privately, and said, "Oh, this made me think of my own story, my own story of light. It made me stop focusing on myself and my family so much and think about other people." And so, I felt people had the stories to tell. And we think that that will help *us*, I think, reading these people's stories and working with them to see what insights, what lights, they can find at these moments. Because they're there; we just, as we've said before, need to train ourselves to look for them, to exercise that muscle.

CP: And it strikes me that the way that you're doing it is with depth, because sometimes it can seem trite to say to people who are going through really hard times, which a *lot* of people are going through right now, to say "Stay positive, things will..." You know? That doesn't always resonate with someone who is either sick or scared of getting sick, can't leave their house, a caretaker, lost their job, home schooling their kids. I mean, Erik, you're talking about wildfires. New York's going through a devastating period right now. I mean, there's just, it's state to state. Erik, you could go through thousands and thousands of stories, *but,* when you talk about, when you frame it the way the two of you have, it seems to me that it has more depth, and you're not saying, "Stay positive." What you're saying is, "Shift your perspective, if at all possible, within the confines of the twenty-four hour period that we all have ahead of us, God willing. Shift your perspective." That, I think, is really powerful.

MJ: Yeah, and I think it's—Erik, I don't mean to speak for you—but both Erik and I come from families who have gone through a lot. One side of my family was here immersed in the epicenter of World War II, and the stories my grandmother and my father used to tell me, I mean *terrible* things happened, but they told me such funny stories. I heard about the terrible things, and some of it's screened out that I've since put things together, but there are so many funny, jokey stories, humor that they found at different points that I—it just strikes me sometimes like, wow! As an adult, I can't believe what they went through! I can't believe my grandmother's fear for her child. I can't believe it all, and yet she still found the humor. She still found that kind of connection with people. And so, I feel like we want to do this as humans, and these selections help document some of those stories so that they're not lost. And that we can all benefit from them.

CP: Thank you so much, Maria. And where can people submit to the both of you to be considered for your second book?

MJ: We have—and we can share this link with you—if they go to Palamedes Publishing, and then click on the "Finding Light" text icon, there'll be a category or tab that says "Submissions." Does that sound right, Erik? And the link is there?

EP: Yeah, it's just palamedes.pub. That's the website and you can find all the information there. And it would be great to put the actual direct link to the column on the podcast website.

CP: Yes, we will definitely do that, and we'll include that on our website as well inspiredmedia360.com. Erik, I want to leave you with the final word for those people who, no doubt, have enjoyed listening to this interview and maybe are thinking about looking at things with a little bit more light. What would you like to leave them with?

EP: Well, I wanted to make one point about what you said about "stay positive," that trite kind of comment. The reason that that doesn't work is because it's someone who is not having the tragedy experience talking to someone who is and saying "stay positive." And that's patronizing, right? This is more from the first person. So you're the one with the experience getting told to yourself. You're not getting it told to you or forced on you or ordered to do that. It is your own experience. And so to the people who want to submit: you write about your own experience. No one is telling you what you should—you know, "Be happy" or be whatever. "Stay positive." That's not what we're saying. You tell us the experience that you've had and show us how it's transformed you, and there's nothing that anyone can say about that. It's yours.

CP: I love that. That's so important. I want to thank you both so much for spending some time with us today. We'll put up all the information along with this podcast, and best of luck to you as you continue on this endeavor with your second book.

MJ: Thank you. Thank you very much. Thank you for having us.

EP: Thank you very much.

CP: And Maria, good luck to you, professor, and say hi to my friend Lisa when you see her around campus, if you guys are allowed to come in the same room with one another.

MJ: I'll send her a long text.

CP: Ok, perfect. You guys take care. Thank you so much.

MJ: Thank you very much.

EP: Thank you very much.

CP: And thanks for listening everyone. I'm Carey Peña. Again you can find all of our shows and content at inspiredmedia360tv.com. Take care.

Acknowledgements

This collection developed over a difficult period during which we faced many challenges: the obvious one, the pandemic, and many private, individual ones. The editors thank the patience and dedication of our contributors as well as our community of readers.

Erik thanks those who provided feedback on his essay: Alexia, Christie, Kathy, Lloyd, Maria, and Morgan.

Maria dedicates her work to her mother, Margaret L. Jerinic, a reader and writer who would have been first in line to read a copy of this work. Our sudden loss revealed just how many friends she had touched in her life.

About the Authors

Ariana Incorvati graduated *magna cum laude* with a Bachelors of Science in Nursing degree from Salve Regina University. She has spent the first two years of her career working at a major city hospital in the heart of Boston, Massachusetts. As a new graduate nurse on the frontlines of a global pandemic, she has found great comfort in writing as a way to share and reflect on her experiences.

Amir Farid is a physician specializing in cardiovascular medicine. When the pandemic started, he was practicing in a busy metropolitan hospital and fully immersed in the fluid nature of medicine in the flood of COVID-19. However, he currently practices cardiology in a rural setting, where he enjoys caring for patients with complex medical conditions, the beautiful sunny environment in the daytime, and crystal clear sky at night. In his free time, enjoys reading poetry and trying new caffeinated kinds of tea.

Carlos Hiraldo is a Professor of English at the City University of New York. A poet and essayist born and raised in Manhattan, he now lives in Queens with his wife and kids.

Before writing, **Eric Roberson** was a marine infantryman, patrol officer, an internal affairs detective, army civil affairs team sergeant, and a sex crimes detective sergeant. He deployed during the first gulf war and again in 2012, to Afghanistan. After his police and military career, he earned an MFA in creative writing from Augsburg University. Eric writes screenplays and audio dramas in the horror and crime genre. He and his wife and their old hound dog, Blue, live in Southern Nevada near their four grown children, and a crazy and eclectic family of friends and creatives. During the pandemic he partnered with his son to write The Unnatural: An Audio Drama Podcast. Their work can be found at www.hermitsnookproductions.com.

Erik Pihel (pronounced *peel*) wrote *Manhattan*, a short epic poem about New York City, and co-edited the series *Finding Light in Unexpected Places*. "All in All" is an excerpt from his memoir *Nataraja's Dance: Cancer and Self-Realization*, forthcoming in 2023. He has a PhD in English, an MA in Creative Writing, and a black belt in Shotokan karate, and has been programming software for two decades. You can find more information at ErikPihel.com and send feedback to ErikPihel@protonmail.com.

Ivana Cvejic is the Co-Founder and CEO of Renhead and Founder of Paul Andrews International, two Las Vegas-based corporations specializing in Talent and Workforce Management solutions. She is known best for large scale buildouts, restructuring of departments to increase efficiencies post mergers and innovating new workforce strategies for large corporations within all sectors. She graduated Magna Cum Laude from the University of California, Riverside with a BA in English Literature. She grew up in Los Angeles, CA and lives between Las Vegas and New York with her husband. She's involved in charitable organizations focused on education, children's welfare and diversity initiatives in the workplace. She is an active mentor and coach for hundreds of professionals and is an active investor and advisor in over a dozen firms focused on human capital, technology, real estate, healthcare, consumer/retail and energy sectors.

James Roderick Burns's fiction has appeared in *The Dead Mule School of Southern Literature*, *La Piccioletta Barca*, and *The Yorkshire Journal*. His story "Trapper" (*Funicular Magazine*) was nominated for Pushcart 2020, and his first collection of short stories, *Beastly Transparencies*, is due from Eyewear in 2021. He lives in Edinburgh and serves as Deputy Registrar General for Scotland.

Kerri Younger is a 37-year-old mother to two boys. She currently works as a Project Manager for BAE Systems in the Submarines sector. She has a previous published story "The Lost and Found" as part of the *Far Worlds Anthology*. Her hobbies include reading books and watching films, as well as going out for walks in the Lake District, which is only half an hour from her home. She has always had a love of writing but has the aspiration for it to be her full-time role. She is at her most chilled and relaxed when she is sat with a good book and a strong coffee.

Laura Valdez Pagliaro, PhD, began her expat journey in 2003 when she moved from NYC to Rome. Since then, she has traveled and lived abroad with her husband and their two sons, mainly in Europe and the Middle East, but also parts of Latin America and Africa, and a little bit of Asia. She is a writer and educator who has taught writing and literature at American schools and universities in Kuwait and Cairo. Grateful for those who made each place beautiful and enriching beyond measure, she remains rooted to her home on the U.S.-Mexican border.

Margot Douaihy, PhD, is the author of four books, including the true-crime poetry project *Bandit/Queen: The Runaway Story of Belle Starr* (Clemson University Press, 2022). Douaihy teaches Creative Writing and Editing/Publishing at Franklin Pierce University where she serves as the editor of *Northern New England Review* and a section editor of the *Journal of Creative Writing Studies*.

Maria Jerinic teaches in the UNLV Honors College where she offers classes in writing, 18th and 19th century British literature, pedagogy and creative nonfiction. Her scholarship and creative nonfiction have appeared in a variety of print and digital publications.

Trisha Paul is a pediatric oncologist and palliative care physician in training and a writer. She is passionate about caring for her little free library, dancing barefoot, and anything made of cork.

Recent Publications

- Finding Light in Unexpected Places, Volume 1: An Anthology of Surprises
- Gill Puckridge, Gillybean in China: The Adventures of a Wandering Sexagenarian, follow Gillybean's childlike response to turning sixty
- Ingrid Arulaid, StepMOMs' Infinite Love, a children's book where the pain of divorce is overcome by magical love
- Carlos Hiraldo, Machu Picchu Me, urban poems growing into mountains
- Erik Pihel, Manhattan, a mini-epic poem about New York City
- Tavius Dyer, Shadow Work, poems that take the reader from darkness to recovery

Classic Ebooks

- A Gathering Darkness: 13 Classic English Ghost Stories
- Tradition Digitized: Ancient Poems in Modern Streams
- Joseph Conrad, Heart of Darkness
- Stephen Crane, The Red Badge of Courage: An Episode of the American Civil War
- James Joyce, Dubliners
- D. H. Lawrence, The Border Line: Soldier Stories by D. H. Lawrence

CPSIA information can be obtained
at www.ICGtesting.com
Printed in the USA
BVHW041329240222
630007BV00013B/693